Beyond Global Food Supply Chains

Victoria Stead • Melinda Hinkson
Editors

Beyond Global Food Supply Chains

Crisis, Disruption, Regeneration

palgrave
macmillan

Editors
Victoria Stead
Alfred Deakin Institute for Citizenship and Globalisation
Deakin University
Burwood, VIC, Australia

Melinda Hinkson
School of Humanities and Social Sciences
Deakin University
Melbourne, VIC, Australia

Institute of Postcolonial Studies
North Melbourne, VIC, Australia

ISBN 978-981-19-3154-3 ISBN 978-981-19-3155-0 (eBook)
https://doi.org/10.1007/978-981-19-3155-0

This Palgrave Macmillan imprint is published by the registered company Springer Nature Singapore Pte Ltd.
The registered company address is: 152 Beach Road, #21-01/04 Gateway East, Singapore 189721, Singapore

Contents

Notes on Contributors

Jon Altman is an economic anthropologist whose research has focused on the food sovereignty rights of Indigenous people in remote Australia over four decades. He is an emeritus professor at the School of Regulation and Global Governance, The Australian National University.

Alex Blanchette is an anthropologist at Tufts University whose research examines shifting values of human labour, non-human life and industrialization and deindustrialization in the United States. He is the author of *Porkopolis: American Animality, Standardized Life, and the Factory Farm* (2020)

Maggie Dickinson is Assistant Professor of Interdisciplinary Studies at Guttman Community College, CUNY. Her book *Feeding the Crisis: Care and Abandonment in America's Growing Food Safety Net* examines welfare policy, inequality and the politics of redistribution.

Kelly Donati is an ethnographer in gastronomy and agriculture. She coordinates and lectures in Australia's only bachelor of food studies and master of food systems and gastronomy at William Angliss Institute in Melbourne.

Tomaso Ferrando is a research professor at the Faculty of Law (Law and Development Research Group) and Institute of Development Policy (IOB), University of Antwerp (Belgium). Between 2016 and 2020, he was legal advisor of the former UN Special Rapporteur on the Right to Food, Professor Hilal Elver.

David Boarder Giles is Lecturer in Anthropology at Deakin University. His book, *A Mass Conspiracy to Feed People: Food Not Bombs and the World-Class Waste of Global Cities* (2021), explores the ways in which discarded surpluses—of people, places and things—are circulated in "global" cities.

Matthew Henry is Associate Professor of Planning at Massey University in the School of People, Environment and Planning. His research focuses on the historical technopolitics of agri-food systems and environmental knowledge.

Melinda Hinkson is Associate Professor of Anthropology at Deakin University and director of the independent Institute of Postcolonial Studies, North Melbourne. Her most recent work is an ethnography of displacement, *See How We Roll: Enduring Exile Between Desert and Urban Australia* (2021). Melinda's new research explores transformations in the agricultural sector and complexities in relationships between residents of metropolitan and rural places.

Daren Shi-Chi Leung has completed his PhD, "Farming as Method: Contextualising the Politics of Food and Farming in South China", at the University of Sydney. His research deploys a socio-metabolic lens to rethink food politics in relation to the historical transformation of China and the shifting geopolitics in Asia.

Francis Markham is a research fellow at the Centre for Aboriginal Economic Policy Research (CAEPR) at The Australian National University. His research aims to integrate critical geographic theory with quantitative methods, in particular the social applications of Geographic Information Systems (GIS).

Christopher Mayes is a research fellow in the Alfred Deakin Institute at Deakin University and research-affiliate in Sydney Health Ethics at the University of Sydney. He is the author of *The Biopolitics of Lifestyle: Foucault, Ethics, and Healthy Choices* (2016) and *Unsettling Food Politics: Agriculture, Dispossession and Sovereignty in Australia* (2018).

Carolyn Morris is Senior Lecturer in Sociocultural Anthropology at Massey University in Aotearoa New Zealand. Her research and teaching interests are in cultures of agriculture and the politics of food, with interests in ethnicity, gender, rurality and race relations.

Kirstie Petrou is a human geographer and research associate at the Climate and Sustainability Policy Research Group (CASPR), Flinders University. She is the author of *If Everyone Returned, the Island Would Sink: Urbanisation and Migration in Vanuatu.*

Lauren Rickards is a professor in the School of Global Urban and Social Studies at RMIT University, Melbourne, where she leads the climate change transformations research programme. Lauren is also a co-director of the Climate Change Exchange and a lead author with the Intergovernmental Panel on Climate Change.

Angie Sassano is a PhD candidate in the Alfred Deakin Institute at Deakin University, investigating the decolonization of alternative food movements. She is an interdisciplinary researcher with interests in food ethics and biopolitics.

Sarah Ruth Sippel is a senior researcher at the Leipzig University, Germany. Her research explores the nexus between global food security, financialization of natural resources and emerging forms of solidarities within global agri-food systems.

Victoria Stead is an anthropologist and Australian Research Council DECRA senior research fellow in the Alfred Deakin Institute for Citizenship and Globalisation, Deakin University. Her research sits at the intersection of attention to race and labour relations, land and landscape, and the reverberations of (post)coloniality in Australia and across Australia–Pacific relations. She is the author of *Becoming Landowners: Entanglements of Custom and Modernity in Papua New Guinea and Timor-Leste* (2017) and editor, with Jon Altman, of *Labour Lines and Colonial Power: Indigenous and Pacific Islander Labour Mobility in Australia* (2019).

List of Figures

Introduction

ADI
ALFRED DEAKIN INSTITUTE FOR CITIZENSHIP AND GLOBALISATION

DEAKIN UNIVERSITY

ACADEMY OF THE SOCIAL SCIENCES IN AUSTRALIA

IPCS.
THE INSTITUTE OF POSTCOLONIAL STUDIES.

PART I

Foundations

CHAPTER 1

Introduction: Beyond Global Supply Chains

Melinda Hinkson and Victoria Stead

Abstract Global food supply chains, we have been told often in recent years, are in crisis. How much, though, does this language of crisis—as particular, contextual, temporally bound—suffice to describe the conditions of the present? This chapter, and the book it introduces, take the COVID-19 pandemic as a springboard to interrogate a larger set of structural, environmental and political fault lines running through the global food system. In a context in which disruptions to the production, distribution and consumption of food are figured as exceptions to the smooth, just-in-time efficiencies of global supply chains, we examine the pandemic not simply as a particular and acute moment of disruption but rather as a lens on a deeper, longer set of structural processes within which disruption is endemic. At a time when it is more likely to be grasped in terms of

M. Hinkson (✉)
School of Humanities and Social Sciences, Deakin University,
Melbourne, VIC, Australia

Institute of Postcolonial Studies, North Melbourne, VIC, Australia
e-mail: melinda.hinkson@deakin.edu.au

V. Stead
Alfred Deakin Institute for Citizenship and Globalisation, Deakin University,
Burwood, VIC, Australia
e-mail: victoria.stead@deakin.edu.au

V. Stead, M. Hinkson (eds.), *Beyond Global Food Supply Chains*,
https://doi.org/10.1007/978-981-19-3155-0_1

speculative investment than as a common good, food offers a vital prism for grappling with the logics by which power circulates in the world. Attending to this constellation of forces calls for attention to supply chains as key mechanisms in the organization of the capitalist food system but also demands that we extend our thinking beyond the bounded linearities of supply chain models.

Keywords Capitalist food system • Crisis • Disruption • Supply chains • COVID-19 • Regeneration

Global food supply chains, we have been told often in recent years, are in crisis. Beginning in March 2020, the COVID-19 pandemic's myriad impacts on human life included dramatic and far-reaching disruptions to global food systems. Border closures triggered critical labour shortages for crop harvesting; outbreaks of infection spread through abattoirs and processing facilities; panic buying cleared supermarket shelves; the precariousness of hospitality and gig-economy work was amplified. Now, as this book goes to press, Russia's invasion of Ukraine is prompting new warnings of crisis, with delays, price-hikes and shortages in the global food supply chain forecast as oil and gas prices rice and as access to the Russian raw material exports needed for the production of fertilizers plummets. Speaking to the BBC, head of global fertilizer corporation Yara International has declared, "For me, it's not whether we are moving into a global food crisis—it's how large the crisis will be" (Simpson, 2022). How much, though, does this language of crisis—as particular, contextual, temporally bound—suffice to describe the conditions of the present? In the case of the COVID-19 pandemic, it has also been clear that the virus' spread exposed fault lines that run farther and deeper than the circumstances of the pandemic itself, highlighting the nature of a global food system that both relies upon and reproduces acute inequalities of risk, vulnerability, hunger, wealth and power. To this end, the pandemic revealed the global food system as not simply *in* a state of particular and acute disruption but rather as *itself* inherently disruptive—of human lives and flourishing, of relationships between people, places and ecologies.

This collection of essays takes the upheaval of the pandemic as a springboard from which to interrogate a larger set of structural, environmental and political fault lines running through the global food system. In a context in which disruptions to the production, distribution and consumption of food are figured as exceptions to the smooth, just-in-time efficiencies of global supply chains, the chapters that follow examine the pandemic not simply as a particular and acute moment of disruption but rather as a lens on a deeper, longer set of structural processes within which disruption is endemic. Here, as Alex Blanchette describes in the Afterword to this collection, drawing on Victoria Stead and Kirstie Petrou's chapter, the global food system is one constantly scrambling to patch the very cracks and weaknesses it reproduces. Similarly, while we do attend here to the various expressions and temporalities of crisis in this system, we heed those who have cautioned of the immobilizing and obfuscatory framings of "crisis" as exception (Roitman, 2014). The vulnerabilities and inequalities produced as part of business-as-usual in the global food system have been intensified and rendered newly visible by COVID-19, but this intensification has also shone new light on transformational possibilities.

Extending beyond the bounded linearities of supply-chain models, there is a complex constellation of forces that traverse and govern food systems, from the transnational workings of UN, World Trade Organization and European Union committees to the accelerating influence of transnational agri-investors; to the industrialization of production and pressures to intensify and expand the scale of farming; to the fragility of migrant labour markets exposed by prolonged international border closures; and the determined push-back of small-scale regenerative farming, food sovereignty and cooperative movements. Threading through all of these intersecting issues is a set of intensifying pressures associated with environmental destruction, loss of biodiversity and the complex of impacts associated with climate change, rising temperatures and unreliable water supply—all of which are forcing growers and policymakers alike to confront the need for change.

To grasp the food system in its complexity forces us to confront fundamental questions, including, for example, whether the farm is the logical place to start any enquiry in relation to food. Or, in other words, where do supply chains begin? And (where) do they end? In asking such questions, this collection seeks to speak with, and build upon, the critical scholarship of Anna Tsing on "supply chain capitalism" and others who have similarly drawn attention to the cultural and political logics within which supply chains and capitalist value are necessarily embedded (Bear et al., 2015; Tsing, 2009, 2016). However, we also seek to extend beyond the supply chain frame—in its critical as well as traditional modes—to the sprawling constellations of power, materiality and entangled life that necessarily exceed it. At a time when food is more likely to be grasped in terms of speculative investment than as a common good, this book proposes it as a vital prism for grappling with the logics by which power circulates in the world. Attention to food—along the supply chain, and beyond its edges—sheds light on the complex workings and failures of colonial capitalism, on escalating climate change, on the reproduction of hunger and structural exclusion, and on alternative regimes of value that would anchor food and feeding firmly back on the ground.

This collection of essays has its origins in a workshop sponsored by the Academy of the Social Sciences in Australia and co-hosted by the Alfred Deakin Institute for Citizenship and Globalisation, Deakin University and the Institute of Postcolonial Studies, Melbourne, in June 2021, in the midst of an extended COVID-19 lockdown. The pandemic has been, then, both an empirical touchstone for the collection and the context within which the chapters were produced. Most contributions engage the pandemic directly; some take other of the food system's disruptions as their focus. They are grouped under four themes.

"Foundations" includes this introductory overview, which is followed by Lauren Rickards and Melinda Hinkson's exploration of global supply chains as artefacts of distinctive social formations and conduits of colonial capital power. Supply chains are, they argue, ultimately disruptive mechanisms that separate people from places, from each other and from the very idea of the production of food for nourishment. Sarah Ruth Sippel's reading of the recent boom in agri-investment then offers another perspective on the underpinnings of contemporary, global food relations. Tracking patterns of investment with origins in the 2007/08 financial crisis, Sippel shows how the "winners" from that crisis are now consolidating their power, and profits, through the pandemic.

"Production" opens with Victoria Stead and Kirstie Petrou's examination of the pandemic's disruptive impact on labour in the Australian horticultural industry. They show that attempts to deal with a shortage of seasonal workers resulted in a paradoxical entrenchment of uneven distributions of precarity, risk and vulnerability along the fault lines of race and migration status. Kelly Donati, working in the Western Australian wheat belt, and Daren Shi-Chi Leung in southern China provide compelling case studies of transformational farming projects across scale that draw creatively on diverse regenerative and traditional agrarian techniques. Both cases suggest cautious optimism, revealing considerable scope for creative working with, and pushing back against, the organizing logic of global capital.

The chapters gathered under "Distribution" explore instances of the pandemic's impact on food supply and accessibility. Matthew Henry and Carolyn Morris unpack the "crisis" of essential food shortages. Through case studies of disrupted supplies of pork and flour in Aotearoa New Zealand, they expose the fantasies of logistics through attention to the social, material and affective liveliness of actual substances. Maggie Dickinson analyses the United States' mass mobilization of food-aid programmes, demonstrating that in the face of escalating unemployment and life-threatening risks for frontline food workers, hunger continues to be used to entrench unsafe working situations that prop up a racist and ecologically destructive food system. David Boarder Giles presents an intimate perspective on the pandemic supermarket through ethnographic attention to the labour undertaken by essential workers in an inner-city independent grocery store. His chapter casts light on the supermarket as at once a definitive node of the global food supply chain and a key site for the expropriation, circulation and accumulation of surplus value.

In the final section, "Food Politics", Jon Altman and Francis Markham take us to the remote Indigenous communities of northern Australia, where a food security "crisis" is shown to be primarily an artefact of government policies designed to punish the poor and push remote-community residents to urban centres. Government responses to the pandemic paradoxically offered a reprieve for these exceptionally governed citizens and hence shed light on the basic structural reforms that could readily alleviate hunger and misery into the future. Tomaso Ferrando takes us to the UN Food Systems Summit, where transnational corporate actors intervene with state support to distance peasants, Indigenous communities and citizens from vital decisions in relation to global agriculture. Finally, we move from the theatre of the UN to quotidian experiences of consumption, where Christopher Mayes and Angie Sassano critically explore the limitations of consumer-food-ethics campaigns. The collection is rounded out by Alex Blanchette's Afterword. In reflecting upon the ever-compounding brutalizing history of agricultural capitalism, Blanchette draws on the concept of "temporary measures" as a way of coming at the "non-transformational upheavals" upon which contributors to this collection reflect. Drawing on the work of Silvia Federici, and her rejection of the characterization of capitalism as a historical break with feudalism, Blanchette offers the ultimately hopeful vision of capitalism itself as a temporary measure—one of many patches on the structural weaknesses of the global food system and the relations of power it embodies. So conceived, this temporary measure might yet be overcome by people in the pursuit of fuller visions of nourishment and vitality, through a profoundly different set of attitudes to the production of food and practices of feeding.

References

Bear, L., Ho, K., Tsing, A. L., & Yanagisako, S. (2015, March 30). Gens: A feminist manifesto for the study of capitalism. *Fieldsights*. https://culanth.org/fieldsights/gens-a-feminist-manifesto-for-the-study-of-capitalism

Roitman, J. (2014). *Anti-Crisis*. Duke University Press.

Simpson, E. (2022). Ukraine war "catastrophic for global food". *BBC*. Retrieved March 22, from https://www.bbc.com/news/business-60623941

Tsing, A. (2009). Supply chains and the human condition. *Rethinking Marxism, 21*(2), 148–176.

Tsing, A. (2016). What is emerging? Supply chains and the remaking of Asia. *The Professional Geographer, 68*(2), 330–337.

CHAPTER 2

Supply Chains as Disruption

Lauren Rickards and Melinda Hinkson

Abstract In this chapter, we explore supply chains with an interest in the complex conjunctions of practice, values and effects that their underpinning modernist imaginary of "seamless circulation" precludes from view. The agricultural landscapes of northwest Victoria provide a compelling vantage from which to ground truth and trouble the idea of seamless circulation and relatedly the idea that disruptions are merely technical blips in otherwise well-oiled machines. Working between the interpretive lenses of Anna Tsing and Bernard Stiegler, supply chains emerge as artefacts of distinctive social formations, conduits of colonial capital power, and ultimately distancing mechanisms that separate people from places and each other. Yet supply chains are also imperfect and incomplete in their operations, and it is this observation that provides for creative responses and the

L. Rickards (✉)
Centre for Urban Research, RMIT University, Melbourne, VIC, Australia
e-mail: lauren.rickards@rmit.edu.au

M. Hinkson
School of Humanities and Social Sciences, Deakin University, Melbourne, VIC, Australia

Institute of Postcolonial Studies, North Melbourne, VIC, Australia
e-mail: melinda.hinkson@deakin.edu.au

V. Stead, M. Hinkson (eds.), *Beyond Global Food Supply Chains*,
https://doi.org/10.1007/978-981-19-3155-0_2

hope of reinvigorating more grounded approaches to the production of food and practices of feeding.

Keywords Agriculture • Supply chains • Scale • Disruption • Australia

In the Shadowlands of Supply Chains

Driving through northwest Victoria in late summer, you will encounter endless horizons of thick green and white plastic sheeting rolled out across rows of vines, protecting first-class table grapes from the remote but consequential possibility of hail. Expensive and unwieldly, not to mention environmentally unfriendly, this prophylactic securitization of grapes is viewed by (large) farmers as an increasingly necessary protection against the risk of damaged crops and resultant drops in their price. Across this landscape, there are many such techniques to guard against risks. These risks extend beyond those communicated with growing urgency by climate scientists. They are mediated and created by markets and their broader political economies.

There are many recent incidents across this landscape of farmers ploughing fully ripened crops and the related financial investment back into the earth. In one case, 40 acres of celery was sacrificed, as no pickers were available to harvest the crop at a fee that would make the process profitable. In another, a plantation of watermelons met the same fate when the large supermarket to whom the farmer was contracted suddenly dropped its purchasing price by 50 per cent in response to an unseasonably cool summer—consumer interest in the fruit had plummeted, yet there was no change in the shelf price. In another case, crops of oranges had been downgraded, diverted to juice as a result of skin discolouration caused by wind rubbing fruit against fruit. According to Australia's National Crop Loss Register, 85,000 agricultural businesses reported significant crop losses within a few months of COVID-19 arriving. Millions of dollars' worth of crops were left rotting in the fields (Liveris, 2020), rendering worthless and invisible the huge amounts of water, fertilizer, and pesticides invested in them and the large environmental costs imposed in their name.

In the wheat-belt area, pesticides are an especially key input in most cropping systems, particularly given the turn to water-saving but synthetic chemical-reliant "no-till" cropping systems. The main active chemical is glyphosate. Despite being the focus of various lawsuits about its deadly health and ecological impacts, glyphosate remains a basic ingredient of pesticide mixes, with two-thirds produced *en masse* in specialized industrial manufacturing zones in China, like many of the chemicals that Australian industries are reliant on (Productivity Commission, 2021). Chinese glyphosate factory production was disrupted by COVID-19's effects on the upstream production of raw materials (e.g. glycine), labour shortages and transport blockages, right when Australian farmers' desire for it escalated as favourable post-drought rainfall fuelled their optimism about the next season. Desperate searches to source it led to many farmers paying sky-high prices (McNaughton, 2020). Invisible to most of us, this disruption of crop inputs was one stark reminder of the many long, hidden, just-in-time supply chains that Australian agriculture is reliant on and vulnerable to. Seemingly a "black swan" event, the pandemic has made visible threatening possibilities previously unimagined.

At least, that is how it appeared. While the pandemic has indeed awoken urban public awareness of supply chain disruption, for farmers and others in Australian agriculture the assumption that supply chains flow smoothly and securely has never held. For those supplying Australia's highly concentrated and export-oriented agricultural markets, supply chains are as much a fickle master as they are a benevolent servant. The small vignettes rehearsed above might be interpreted as disruptions, but we offer them as indications of the kinds of rupture that are endemic to the Australian agricultural system—the small sacrifices required on a daily basis in Australian farming to ensure the pre-eminence of global supply chains. In this chapter, we approach supply chains as complex conjunctions of practice, values and effects that their underpinning modernist imaginary of "seamless circulation" precludes from view.

Scaling

Central to the sociological significance of global supply chains is their ambitious reach and scale (Tsing, 2012a). As Anna Tsing argues, scalability is "the ability to expand—and expand, and expand—without rethinking basic elements". Like a house of mirrors, scalability "allows us to see only uniform blocks, ready for further expansion" (Tsing, 2012b). But behind its endless refractions, scalability is characterized by sharp differentiations and divisions, "a triumph of precision design" (Tsing, 2012b, p. 143). Only very carefully selected parts of the world are allowed into the enclosed chains of connectivity that whisk their offerings through blanked landscapes, towns and seas to the next special destination, leaving the unchosen to only watch the constant stream of B-double trucks, planes and ships. Scalability is a triumph precisely because it differentiates itself from the myriad singular, non-scalable biological, cultural and social forms that otherwise make up the diversity of the world (Tsing, 2012a).

How scalability is done and how supply chains are constructed across borders is itself diverse, with fine-grained qualitative distinctions characterizing the choices and transactions made. Deeply cultured relations differently organize reciprocal exchanges, trade routes and circuits of goods. For example, *British* supply chains of green beans privilege homogeneity in beans, whereas *French* ones privilege regional distinctiveness in beans (Freidberg, 2004). Whether British or French, the national identity of such chains refers to their consumer and corporate base, not their spatial extent. Each supply chain retraces colonial passages and reinforces the magnetic pull of resources and capital to the Global North. As Tsing observes, far from being new or modern, the ideal of scalability originates in the sixteenth-century plantation and the racialized forms of dispossession and labour exploitation upon which it turned (and continues to turn): slavery (Tsing, 2012a). Colonization was a process of establishing, securing and scaling supply chains. These chains are thus an artefact and a vehicle of colonial capitalism, remaining today, beneath their shiny digital signs, what Chickasaw scholar Jodi Byrd (2011) might describe as *the transit of empire.*

As much as colonizing spaces, supply chains have colonized minds. Today the ideal of linking into international markets remains a common marker of success in modern business. Here, the appeal of finely threaded supply chains snaking horizontally across the world merges in the mind with the ideal of jumping scales from local to national to global, even to universal. How to take innovation "to scale" is a profitable new area of expertise. Farmers are targeted as not just potential adopters of the vision but potential consumers of the myriad tools and technologies that promise to help them scale their own businesses, from the precision agricultural machinery that allows them to carve paddocks into laser-graded units, to the smart farming sensors that monitor soil moisture from outer space, to the phone apps that report real-time movements in commodity prices and shipping containers, to the banking credit that can fund it all, for a fee. Governments are also targeted, in recognition that scaling out across the farming population requires "scaling up" the right settings into policies, structures and decision making, cultivating a regulatory environment and innovation system conducive (only) to the right types of suppliers and buyers.

Differentiating

Scaling is not only about homogenization. To create the gradients along which capital and goods flow, heterogeneity is essential. Supply chains, then, are not just about connection; they are about "difference-in-connection" (Tsing, 2016). They generate "global integration, on the one hand", and "diverse niches, on the other" (Tsing, 2009). Crucially, such diversity is not celebrated for its own sake; it is ranked and used to fuel competition. The products, suppliers and areas ushered into global supply chains are not selected by their absolute characteristics but by their *relative* ones—they are the ones that are favoured at that particular moment in time. Although other places, products and people are simply blanked out in depictions of supply chains stretched purposively across the globe, they lurk in background calculations of possible future options, a reminder to the linked-in few to keep performing. If one is unable to deliver products on time and to a set standard, it places one's *future* as well as one's immediate income at risk because it marks one as unreliable. If a buyer has to go elsewhere for a product, even for a short-term disruption, there is no guarantee they will return.

Reflecting the nation's colonial roots, Australia has long taken pride in exporting goods to overseas consumers, as if others' acceptance of our material offerings signals a far deeper belonging than just inclusion in a supply chain. Underpinning such a preoccupation are abstract modernist notions of global prestige and international competition. For countries such as Australia (or, as Ilppo Soininvaara discusses, Finland) that are somewhat unsure of their global standing, such an imaginary drives a fierce ranking of subnational regions, determining which parts of the nation are considered the "key national spaces … where global competitiveness is performed" (Soininvaara, 2021, pp. 10, 11). The resultant spatial hierarchies reflect and attract the paths of global supply chains. They also reflect urban-centrism, which remains the telos of virtually all such chains. In contrast, rural regions are frequently cast as "troublesome spaces", with few managing to secure global recognition or the attention of international investors or suppliers (Soininvaara, 2021). Rural areas' failure to secure reliable labour perpetuates the image of them as undisciplined and unappealing, both to workers and to those who might enter contractual agreements with businesses in the area. Supply chains, Tsing reminds us, are about *discipline*—of suppliers, workers, logistics and natures. Those who resist or fail to perform risk being quickly replaced. For Australia—that want-to-be island of the Global North within the deep Global South, a nation whose productive capacity has been underpinned by "capital in-flows" from distant shores for over 200 years (Black et al., 2017)—the fear of "capital flight" and the abandonment it represents are visceral.

Revaluing

Increasingly, the value afforded a commodity, business, property or region depends less on its productive capacity or physical merits (even its relative ones) and more on the mysterious whims of the financial world. The magical touch of finance has spread across the globe like a contagion, drawing and continually redrawing global supply chains as powerfully as any etched colonial trade route. Referred to by some as a second wave of colonization, this financial capitalism has financialized myriad aspects of agriculture. By financialization, we mean here the strategy of "profiting without producing" (Lapavitsas, 2013) by exploiting interest rates in loaning and reloaning "fictitious capital": "money that is thrown into circulation as capital without any material basis in commodities or productive activity" (Harvey, 2006, p. 95). Agricultural products are now not only commoditized (i.e. reduced to their market exchange value and sold as one commodity among others—turning food into widgets, as one of our interviewees put it); they have also been colonized by parasitical financial products such as "wheat futures" that put the commodities "in play" in the global economy and in doing so tie their exchange value to innumerable and untraceable financial transactions around the world, twisting and contorting the relationship between their price and the on-ground contexts that produced them. In this way, agricultural production and supply chains have been distorted to supply profit, not food.

Inputs right along agri-food supply chains have been financialized (Clapp, 2014), including water and water infrastructure. For example, whether and how London's water infrastructure provides "for actual needs"—that is, provides potable water to residents—has become less relevant to the company in charge (Thames Water) and its myriad owners (first, Australia's Macquarie Bank, now various sovereign wealth and pension funds in Canada and elsewhere) than whether its future revenue flows can be bundled up as "securities" and sold to other financial actors (Loftus et al., 2019). In this way, the "illiquid assets" of water infrastructure have been turned into "liquid forms" in a financial sense (Pryke & Allen, 2019, p. 2), embedding water infrastructure into a "supply chain" that has little to do with supplying water and everything to do with supplying financial returns.

In the 2008 Global Financial Crisis when the whole overheated web of promises, wishes and transactions came crashing down, the "solid" character of farmland gained appeal as an apparently safe haven for flighty capital (Ouma, 2020, p. 67). Through ongoing "moral struggles" about its inherent values (Ouma, 2020, p. 66), farmland has been turned into a new asset class and bestowed with "legitimate financial worth". In the process, rural and remote areas have been cast once again as a new frontier and a target for investment and speculation. Some of the swelling cohorts of new agri-investors target the distant high-risk environment of the Global South, where farmland can be made fresh out of forest or wasteland. Others prefer the slightly slower profits but greater security of more established contexts such as Australia (Sippel, 2018). To help things along, the Australian government (2021) aggressively markets Australian farmland to investors (e.g. see the new *Why Australia: Benchmark Report 2021* by Austrade). Partly as a result, over the last decade, Australian farmland value has become "red hot" among international investors (Tracey, 2020).

Foreign investment is spreading into conventional family farming districts and through the supply chain to processors, packers, distributors. It is also flowing through the financial supply chain to insurance companies, who offer to offset the risk at every turn, all the while becoming large holders and managers of farmland themselves. All farmland investors are seeking scale, consolidating farm properties into larger and larger parcels. In doing so, the aggregate value of the parcels begins to approximate the smallest financial units that investment firms are accustomed to dealing with (Fairbairn, 2020), the farm operations become more *scalable*, and the farms begin to attract government-subsidized infrastructure.

Whether foreign or Australian owned, much agricultural production today occurs in distinctively corporatized arrangements, whereby owners outsource the production to managers, who in turn tend to outsource most of the practical work to others. This commodification of labour means that those involved are often relatively disconnected from the land, upon which they work but do not live; they are employed to make market-driven decisions, and they work to maximize profits. It is part of a deliberate strategy of achieving consistency across corporate holdings, uncontaminated by local environments, communities and their predilections. As Anna Tsing notes, such self-containment is core to scalability—to being able to "expand without changing", moving "from small to large without redoing the design", thanks to avoiding relationships and their threatening transformative potential (Tsing, 2012b, p. 145).

Infrastructure is another tool of standardization and expansion, allowing supply chains to circulate through farms more swiftly and purposively. On-farm infrastructure also serves another purpose, allowing *capital* to circulate and accumulate in farms more swiftly. Reflecting the hegemonic real estate mantra about capital flowing to the "highest and best use" (Fairbairn, 2020), farmland increases in value as it is "improved"—for example, made more productive and standardized through the addition of new digital agriculture technologies or cavernous sheds. Irrespective of whether such improvements pay off in more profitable production, the financial value of "capitalized" land tends to appreciate, providing investors with their returns on investment and adding to agriculture's appeal as a new asset class. High land values tend to have a "neighbourhood effect", adding value to a general region or even nation. They also attract more middle players, keen to facilitate the supply of land into the market, for a fee.

All of this interest and interference in agriculture from non-agricultural players adds enormous uncertainty to farmers' decision-making. No longer can prices be anticipated using common-sense logics; more factors than are calculable are involved. In paying attention to what farmers do and what they say, we glimpse diverse approaches, some of which feel akin to walking a tightrope. Some of those who stay in the game do so by "running to stand still", securing a position that might be characterized as just beyond hanging on. They are aware that they do their work on constantly shifting ground. It is what anthropologist Henrik Vigh (2009) describes as "motion squared", whereby everything is in a state of motion and volatility, with farmers sharply aware of the constantly intensifying pressures on their margins and the risk of obsolescence.

Others are keenly aware of farmers' uncertainty and pressures. Numerous consultants and digital "decision support tools" offer to help farmers through the maze, while many investment companies offer to relieve farmers of stress by buying them out and reinstating them as a farm manager. But many Australian farmers are determined to remain owners themselves. The country's record land prices reflect not just foreign investors seeking properties to purchase but Australian farmers taking more risk to buy more land. As a rural banker noted recently, many are suffering from FOMO: "People are realising that they've just got to act now, because that parcel of land may not be available for a substantial period of time" (Jasper, 2021). Crucially, increasing farmland value underpins the equity calculations that banks use to offer farmers more credit to purchase more land. It is a cyclical financial equation that has driven Australia's total farm debt to record highs ($86.9 billion) in the last financial year (Australian Government, 2020), effectively handing ownership of more farmland to banks.

Meanwhile, those without land are increasingly unable to break into farming. The size of farm that is considered viable has increased with the purportedly universal law of scalability, and so too has the cost of farmland per hectare. The result is that the "supply" of farmers may be running out, as those without millions in equity are unable to get established, while those within the sector continue to leave (Jasper, 2021), along with their families, community ties, rural services and place-based knowledge.

All of this is invisible at the industry or market level on which policy is focused. Because many Australian farmers produce common products that serve as the raw materials for others' supply chains, their farms are considered broadly commensurable with any other. As such, any disruptions to their contribution, including their entire exit from the sector, barely register, at least if the overall rate of productivity growth continues to climb, as it tends to do if the land is absorbed into larger operations. Relatedly, the Productivity Commission does not rank agriculture as an essential industry. Not only are exported products rarely discussed in anything but coarse economic summations, such as the "record $50.1 billion of Australian agriculture produced in 2019–2020" (Rural Bank, 2020), but also they are part of a supply chain that we now know the federal government does *not* consider to be critical because the products do not directly serve Australian consumers (Productivity Commission, 2021). For the many highly geared family farms straining to enter privileged global circulations, the upshot is that while they are trumpeted as a national success story—Australian farmers are the best in the world! (Hayman & Rickards, 2013)—in other ways, they are relegated to a mere footnote in the ongoing colonization of the planet by supply chain capitalism.

Rupturing

North of Victoria's wheat belt, not far from the expanses of plastic-wrapped grapevines, the landscape is increasingly dominated by almond plantations. Many of them are owned by Hancock Natural Resource Group, owned in turn by Canada's largest insurer, Manulife Investment Management Company, which invests retirement funds for various groups of North American workers (Fairbairn, 2020). Almonds are an increasingly popular crop, especially given demand for lower-carbon milk alternatives, which is proving to be a serious disruption for the dairy industry (Clay et al., 2020). Yet the life cycle analysis (LCA) calculations that rank almond milk as generating lower carbon across its global supply chain relative to equivalent units of dairy milk not only exclude the complexities that make such calculations dubious (Freidberg, 2013) but also overlook most non-carbon considerations. The health, social and ecological disbenefits of thirsty almond plantations upon local ecosystems and communities are severe and highly visible to those who now live in their midst. Such problems are not the fault of almond trees per se but the profit motive they are being put towards. Growing almond trees takes more water even than growing cotton (Davies, 2019), but it makes a certain short-term sense when the market price is so high.

Smaller-scale farmers express awe, anger and despair in relation to investor-operated large almond plantations. One tells eerie stories of the mysterious deaths of countless native birds ("pests"), especially corellas, and the sudden death of a large grove of decades-old eucalypts, allegedly for simply housing the offending birds. The elderly farmer who shares these stories took up long-distance running a long time ago to deal with the day-to-day stress of farming. Running generated the energy required to solve problems. But, he observes, "you need to run 100 kilometres to deal with such horror".

Prosperity and precarity coexist in supply chains, which "make and use difference and ruination—both in human communities and in the natural world" (Tsing, 2016). The almond "boom" in northern Victoria is not likely to last long. Climate change is accelerating, and as a result, rainfall in northern Victoria is becoming less abundant and less reliable (Victorian Government, 2019). Elaborate water infrastructures are being installed to try to squeeze some savings out of the existing system, reducing the amount that is "wasted" by seeping into the environment. "Rolling out" such irrigation modernization is a massive task and requires farmers to get on board. As such, it is disruptive. But disruption by modernization is deeply normalized and invisibilized.

The late French social theorist Bernard Stiegler compels us to approach disruption as nothing short of an epoch-breaking, unprecedented global force. Automated and reticulated society—society in the time of global supply chains—is a "global cause of colossal social disintegration" (Stiegler, 2019, p. 6). Disruption from this perspective is not a condition of technological glitches or failures in a system but *a system itself*. It destroys local culture, and disintegrates and exploits psychosocial energies, as well as equipment, infrastructure and heritage. Disruption, Stiegler argues, renders human will obsolete—it always arrives too late. It destroys affective relations and the processes of intergenerational transmission and translation whereby shared expectations of and orientations towards the future are generated (Stiegler, 2019, pp. 8–10). Such insights would resonate strongly with the growing number of Australian farmers without farms and rural families without neighbours or real communities. So too do they resonate in other places being reshaped by supply chain capitalism. Marc Edelman, for instance, describes the "hollowing out" of the rural United States as corporate-state abandonment has delivered "shredded social fabric". Justified by neoliberal capital logic, social supports are being comprehensively withdrawn, leaving a devastating human toll.

But the view from the ground also tempers Stiegler's critical insights—disruption is not so total nor so spectacular. As Tsing (2012a, p. 36) puts it, "grand schemes never fully colonise the territories upon which they are imposed". In Australia, the colonization of rural landscapes and life by corporate power and its logics is incomplete, revealing the "unstable commitments" that characterize supply chains (Tsing, 2009). The colonization of rural landscapes and life by corporate power is layered upon older, ongoing processes of colonization and dispossession of First Nations people. Indeed, supply chain capitalism exploits pre-existing forms of dispossession, taking advantage of the destruction of spiritual connection to land and water that may otherwise have provided more widespread moral anchorage, guidance and resistance. Yet this is not the end of the story. One response to the developments sketched here is a strong yearning across Australian agricultural communities to learn from and help nurture Aboriginal cultural attitudes and practice. A growing coalition of activist farmers, environmentalists, First Nations people and concerned citizens is promoting a new kind of collective commitment, to urgently prioritize the fundamental health of the Country, water and people. Such alliances offer our best hope of imagining how we might hack and remodel supply chains, and in the process re-embed food production in the activities of feeding and nurturance, in communities and the Country.

References

Australian Government. (2020). *Agricultural lending data 2018–2019.* Department of Agriculture, Water and the Environment.

Australian Government. (2021). *Why Australia: Benchmark report 2021.* Austrade.

Black, S., Chapman, B., & Windsor, C. (2017). Australian capital flows. *Reserve Bank of Australia Bulletin*, June 2017, 1–12.

Byrd, J. (2011). *The transit of empire: Indigenous critiques of colonialism.* University of Minnesota Press.

Clapp, J. (2014). Financialization, distance and global food politics. *The Journal of Peasant Studies, 41*(5), 797–814.

Clay, N., Sexton, A. E., Garnett, T., & Lorimer, J. (2020). Palatable disruption: The politics of plant milk. *Agriculture and Human Values, 37*, 945–962.

Davies, A. (2019). Tough nut to crack: The almond boom and its drain on the Murray-Darling, *The Guardian*, May 26. Retrieved August 13, 2021, from https://www.theguardian.com/australia-news/2019/may/26/tough-nut-to-crack-the-almond-boom-and-its-drain-on-the-murray-darling

Fairbairn, M. (2020). *Fields of gold.* Cornell University Press.

Freidberg, S. (2004). *French beans and food scares: Culture and commerce in an anxious age.* Oxford University Press.

Freidberg, S. (2013). Calculating sustainability in supply chain capitalism. *Economy and Society, 42*(4), 571–596.

Harvey, D. (2006). *The limits to capital.* Verso books.

Hayman, P., & Rickards, L. A. (2013). Drought, climate change, farming and science: The interaction of four privileged topics. In L. Botterill & G. Cockfield (Eds.), *Drought, risk management, and policy: Decision-making under uncertainty* (pp. 47–69). Taylor and Francis.

Jasper, C. (2021). Red-hot market for Australian farmland leaving first home buyers locked out. *ABC News Online*, May 2. Retrieved August 13, 2021, from https://www.abc.net.au/news/2021-05-02/soaring-market-for-australian-farms/100106246

Lapavitsas, C. (2013). *Profiting without producing: How finance exploits us all.* Verso Books.

Liveris, J. (2020). National Lost Crop Register surpasses $45 million in losses at farmgate value due to worker shortage. *ABC News Online*, February 9. Retrieved August 13, 2021, from https://www.abc.net.au/news/rural/2021-02-09/national-lost-crop-register-surpasses-45-million-in-losses/13132274

Loftus, A., March, H., & Purcell, T. F. (2019). The political economy of water infrastructure: An introduction to financialization. *Wiley Interdisciplinary Reviews: Water, 6*, e1326.

McNaughton, J. (2020). Roundup contamination 'unpreventable', world-first glyphosphate research shows. *ABC News online*, March 19. Retrieved August 13, 2021, from https://www.abc.net.au/news/rural/2020-03-19/international-glyphosate-roundup-hotspot-map/12063156

Ouma, S. (2020). This can('t) be an asset class: The world of money management, 'society', and the contested morality of farmland investments. *Environment and Planning A: Economy and Space, 52*, 66–87.

Productivity Commission. (2021). *Vulnerable supply chains: Interim report*. Australian Government.

Pryke, M., & Allen, J. (2019). Financialising urban water infrastructure: Extracting local value, distributing value globally. *Urban Studies, 56*, 1326–1346.

Rural Bank. (2020). *Australian agriculture trade review 2019/20*. Retrieved August 13, 2021, from https://www.ruralbank.com.au/knowledge-and-insights/publications/agricultural-trade/trade-annual-review-20192020/#:~:text=Australia%20exported%20%2450.1%20billion%20worth,cent%20of%20the%20total%20value

Sippel, S. R. (2018). Financialising farming as a moral imperative? Renegotiating the legitimacy of land investments in Australia. *Environment and Planning A: Economy and Space, 50*, 549–568.

Soininvaara, I. (2021). *The spatial hierarchies of a networked state: Historical context and present-day imaginaries in Finland*. Territory, Politics, Governance. https://www.tandfonline.com/doi/full/10.1080/21622671.2021.1918574

Stiegler, B. (2019). *The age of disruption: Technology and madness in computational capitalism*. Polity Press.

Tracey, M. (2020). How much Aussie farmland is foreign owned? *Farm Weekly*, December 28. Retrieved August 13, 2021, from https://www.farmweekly.com.au/story/7067765/how-much-aussie-farmland-is-foreign-owned/

Tsing, A. L. (2009). Supply chains and the human condition. *Rethinking Marxism, 21*, 148–176.

Tsing, A. L. (2012a). *Friction: An ethnography of global connection*. Princeton University Press.

Tsing, A. L. (2012b). On nonscalability: The living world is not amenable to precision-nested scales. *Common Knowledge, 18*, 505–524.

Tsing, A. (2016). What is emerging? Supply chains and the remaking of Asia. *The Professional Geographer, 68*, 330–337.

Victorian Government. (2019). *Victorian climate projections 2019*. Department of Environmental, Water, Land and Planning. Retrieved August 13, 2021, from https://www.climatechange.vic.gov.au/adapting-to-climate-change-impacts/victorian-climate-projections-2019

Vigh, H. (2009). Motion squared: A second look at the concept of social navigation. *Anthropological Theory, 9*(4), 419–438. https://doi.org/10.1177/1463499609356044

CHAPTER 3

Agri-investment Cashing in on COVID-19

Sarah Ruth Sippel

Abstract Global agri-food relationships are continuously changing. However, some periods can be perceived as critical moments when sudden events challenge established patterns and introduce new dynamics within the agri-food system. Many observers identified the food price hikes in 2007/2008 as such a "turning point". The food price hikes were seen as a stark reminder of the fragility and volatility of the global food system and interpreted as signalling a structural crisis in agriculture and its organizational and institutional frameworks. The 2008 crisis produced both winners and losers. Among the winners were institutional investors that started engaging much more actively in the area of productive resources. Roughly ten years later, the COVID-19 pandemic has disrupted global agri-food relationships again, perhaps even more profoundly. This chapter juxtaposes the crises of 2007/2008 and 2020/2021 and explores the role of financial actors within them. It analyses how financial investors, who emerged as powerful actors out of the 2008 crisis, responded to, and dealt with, the COVID-19 crisis. It further investigates how the pandemic has been rhetorically framed, what investment strategies were promoted, and how financial investors anticipate their engagement with agri-food in (post-)pandemic times.

S. R. Sippel (✉)
Institute of Cultural Anthropology, Leipzig University, Leipzig, Germany
e-mail: sippel@uni-leipzig.de

V. Stead, M. Hinkson (eds.), *Beyond Global Food Supply Chains*,
https://doi.org/10.1007/978-981-19-3155-0_3

Keywords Food crisis • Financialization • Agri-food investment • COVID-19

Introduction

Global agri-food relationships are continuously changing. However, some periods are perceived as critical moments when sudden events challenge established patterns and introduce new dynamics within the agri-food system. Many observers identified the food price hikes in 2007/2008 and 2011 as a "turning point" in global agri-food relationships. A decade on, the COVID-19 pandemic has disrupted global agri-food relationships again, perhaps even more profoundly. In this chapter, I juxtapose the crises of 2007/2008 and 2020/2021 and look specifically at the role of financial actors within these. I will address the following questions: how have financial investors—who emerged as new and powerful agri-food actors out of the 2008 crisis—responded to, and dealt with, the COVID-19 crisis? How has the pandemic been rhetorically framed, what kinds of investment strategies have been promoted, and how are financial investors anticipating their engagement with agri-food in (post-)pandemic times?

I begin by briefly outlining how and why financial investors emerged as new players in the agri-food system post-2008. I then outline the response of agri-food investors to the pandemic and suggest that three main arguments can be identified: first, the pandemic is seen as having proven the case for ag-investments by revealing its resiliency in times of crisis; second, the pandemic is presented as a push for further investment in ag- and food-tech; and third, the pandemic is regarded as reinforcing the trend towards increased emphasis on sustainability and climate change within investments. I conclude that while the agri-food investment discourse has broadened to incorporate new areas and issues, its underlying logic of presenting crisis as an opportunity for profit-making remains unchanged.

This chapter is based on analysis of 160 articles on COVID-19 and agricultural investment published on the platform Agri Investor (agriinvestor.com) between March 2020 and July 2021. Agri Investor is a platform providing information on agri-investment, including news on deals, companies, people, and market trends, as well as background analysis and commentary. Agri Investor is a key actor that has been supporting the discursive construction and promotion of agriculture as a financial asset class since 2010 and has also organized events to bring stakeholders together.

The 2008 Food Price Crisis and the Emergence of Financial Actors in Agri-food

In 2008, after two decades of volatile but overall declining food prices, global prices for staple foods such as maize, wheat and rice increased significantly within a few years (Mittal, 2009). The drivers of the price hikes included short- and mid-term factors such as the temporary decline of agricultural production and food stocks, coupled with rising demand, export restrictions and new agro-fuel policies, as well as financial speculation on commodity markets. These factors were embedded within long-term developments such as declining investments in rural areas and state-led re-regulation of agricultural and financial policies (Gertel & Sippel, 2016). Together, the events of 2007/2008 were seen as "a stark reminder of the fragility and volatility of the global food system" (Clapp & Cohen, 2009, p. 1) and interpreted as signalling a structural crisis in agriculture and its organizational and institutional frameworks (McMichael & Schneider, 2011). Introducing their book *Food Systems Failure*, Rosin, Stock and Campbell suggest that the 2007/2008 crisis exposed the "challenge that localized food scarcity, and subsequent popular protest … posed to a shared sense of progress—and some would argue complacency—toward meeting the world's food demands" (Rosin et al., 2012, p. 1). Hence, they conclude that "[c]learly, an ability to feed the global population was proving to be less certain and hunger on a large scale was still a reality" (Rosin et al., 2012, p. 1). As noted by many observers, the food price hikes impacted especially hard on those groups of people who already needed to spend a major part of their income on food—and resulted in "food riots" in numerous urban centres across the Global South (McMichael, 2014, p. 948). At the same time, the increase in food commodity prices also led a number of new actors—who had not previously been present or very active in the agri-food system—to start engaging much more actively in the area of productive resources. Among these actors were state- and finance-backed actors, who were prompted to invest in natural resources—and first and foremost productive farmland—by a combination of food security motives and a search for alternative financial investment opportunities.

Since the early 2000s, and specifically following the financial crisis of 2007/2008, numerous specialized agricultural investment vehicles have been established, taking various legal forms (including private equity funds, hedge funds, real estate management trusts, and private and public companies) and pursuing different farm ownership and management strategies to construct income streams for investors (cf. Daniel, 2012; Fairbairn, 2014, 2020; Bjørkhaug et al., 2018). The interest in productive resources was partly a response to the poor performance of "traditional" asset classes (such as equities and bonds), all of which suffered during the financial crisis. Consequently, investors searched for new "alternative" asset classes providing returns uncorrelated with the "traditional" ones already existing in their portfolios. Agriculture and farmland were promoted as offering this low or negative correlation with traditional assets and positive risk-return characteristics, both of which were seen as adding to the overall performance of financial portfolios. Moreover, and contrary to other asset classes, in financial theory, both appreciation and the productive capacity of land (i.e., the value of its products) constitute the financial value of land. In other words, farmland is seen as both productive *and* appreciating—as "gold with yield" (Fairbairn, 2014). Further "investment fundamentals" for farmland investments were the finite availability of land, combined with the rising demand for food due to prospective population growth. "Food security" was a crucial narrative and appeared as both a motive to legitimize investment in agriculture and an incentive to stimulate capital inflows into agricultural investment funds (Larder et al., 2015).

Never Waste a Crisis? Financial Investors' Response to COVID-19

Given that financial actors' much more intimate engagement with agriculture emerged out of the conjunction of the 2008 crises, how have these actors dealt with the COVID-19 crisis? I now turn to the response of financial investors to the pandemic as reported on the Agri Investor platform. The initial reaction to the COVID-19 outbreak in March 2020 was marked by a certain degree of uncertainty. The global spread of the virus was unprecedented, and early articles report that investors' reactions reflected the newness and unpredictability of this situation. One of the first articles dealing with COVID-19, titled "Coronavirus plays on the mind of agri investors worldwide", reflects this feeling and describes investors as "nervous and cautious" (Kemp, 2020a). The article starts by stating that "the impact of coronavirus played out across global financial markets in the past two weeks, with stock markets tumbling and companies ... issuing warnings about the impact on earnings" (Kemp, 2020a).

The article continues that "agriculture is no exception" and reports that, although investors were not panicking, there was growing concern in the industry about how long the disruption would last. Australian agriculture specifically is seen as vulnerable, due to its dependence on exports, and with China—where the coronavirus originated—being Australia's biggest export market for major commodities. The article also mentions concerns about congestion in supply chains in Southeast Asia, with the risk of product being stuck at ports.

As the COVID-19 pandemic continued over the course of 2020, this initially rather cautious perspective evolved into a much more confident position about the performance of ag-investment. Investments in agriculture are eventually not only presented as "crisis proofed" but are considered to have large potential for post-pandemic times. Three major themes can be identified, which are explored below.

COVID-19 Proves the Case for Ag-investment

The first general theme that can be identified is that COVID-19 is seen as having made the case for ag-investment. As early as late June 2020, Macquarie Infrastructure and Real Assets (MIRA) CEO Elizabeth O'Leary explained that ag-investments were continuing to perform well in comparison to other asset classes: "As we moved through that early fact-finding stage, it became clear that, particularly for investments like ours with a long-term focus and modest levels of leverage, along with the strong production environment in Australia and strong commodity prices, meant that their exposure with us did not warrant any attention beyond the usual levels" (Kemp, 2020b). In a similar vein, in early July 2020, Angus Ingram, investments and partnerships manager at Kilter Rural, is quoted as saying, "In terms of financial performance—because we are primary production, farmland and water managers—we just haven't been exposed to any economic downturn at all [from the coronavirus]. In fact, probably quite the contrary" (Kemp, 2020d). The article states that Kilter Rural's investments, as well as most of the others reported to Agri Investor by ag-fund managers at that point, performed strongly during the COVID-19 crisis. This point is made in comparison to other sectors, which were previously considered "safe investments" and which suffered during the pandemic, from real estate investments in retail, hotel and office space to infrastructure investments in airports.

Thus, some months into the pandemic, COVID-19 is mostly portrayed as showing agriculture's resilience as an asset class and proving the strength of agriculture's investment fundamentals. This resilience is seen as grounded in agriculture being an "essential" sector, as well as its non-correlation to other economic sectors (Kemp, 2020b). The crisis is thus seen as serving to "reaffirm ag as a resilient and uncorrelated asset class" (Ali, 2020b) or, in the words of Growth Farms' managing director David Sackett, "If anything will help prove the thesis that agricultural investments are non-correlated to other asset classes, this is it" (Ali, 2020c). One article further compares the 2020 situation with 2009/2010, when there was a similar fundraising environment as agribusiness's lack of correlation to the broader economy in the aftermath of the financial crisis drove the increase in interest. "Investors very much like that the sectors that we focus on are essential and these businesses have continued in this period [COVID-19]" (Janiec, 2020b). This performance showed that "the underlying investments are uncorrelated to a lot of other asset classes that the investors have exposure to" (Janiec, 2020b). Similar to 2007/2008, food (in)security is presented as another strong fundamental and incentive for ag-investment. For example, we can read that "food security anxieties will be a catalyst for investment", as the pandemic has "heightened the scrutiny with which virtually every nation views its global and domestic food supply chains" (Ali, 2020b).

At the end of 2020, several articles review the year and again the major conclusion is that agriculture has proven itself as "crisis resilient". It is stated that "agriculture as an asset class navigated through 2020 relatively unscathed from the covid-19 crisis" (Corbett, 2020), while another article concludes, "the world needs food and fiber just as much during a pandemic as at any other time" (Kemp, 2020c). This is seen as "a salient lesson for investors that farmland and other food-related assets can be useful, even necessary, parts of a diversified portfolio, helping to pick up the slack when other asset types suffer" (Kemp, 2020c). Ag's resiliency and "fundamental growth drivers" are considered as proven, unless "unnaturally distorted as in the case of trade wars" (Ali, 2020c). In essence, this article concludes, "trade wars are bigger threats than pandemics", referring to both the US–China trade war and Australia's trade disputes with its largest trading partner, China.

COVID-19 as a Push for Ag- and Food-tech Investment

The second key theme is that COVID-19 has exposed the crucial importance and future relevance of digital technologies, which make investment in ag- and food-tech sectors both necessary and lucrative. Three areas are emphasized in particular: the pandemic's push for indoor farming and for labour mechanization, and its impact on food supply chains and consumption more generally.

Regarding the first, indoor ag-tech is presented as having a "sizable runway as many in and outside the industry look toward it as a potential future solution to food scarcity and food supply chain issues" (Szkutak, 2020). Another article in early 2021 explains that indoor farming became the subject of much discussion and investment throughout 2020 as the global food supply chain challenges created by the pandemic led to food security fears: "Indoor farming, both through naturally lit greenhouses and vertical farming operations using LED lighting and sophisticated AI systems, were therefore identified by many as a potential solution for propping up domestic food production" (Ali, 2021). It is further reported that COVID-19 even led state-owned investors to divert their attention away from real assets towards ag-tech, as the threat of a food security crisis made food and ag-focused technology a "small but important" part of investments. Here, an insider from the sovereign wealth fund industry is quoted as saying, "Sophisticated sovereign wealth funds are not looking too much into land anymore. What they are looking into is to add value into the irrigation and processing value chain. That's why we call agtech an evolution of the general industry. We think it's what investors are tending to these days" (Janiec, 2021).

Issues surrounding labour exposed during the pandemic are the second major incentive for investment in agricultural technologies, and notably those helping to reduce labour on farms through automation. As one article states, COVID-19 exposed shortcomings such as the reliance on migrant labour and poor working conditions in food-processing facilities. These, the article suggests, will "largely be solved by increased mechanization and automation". "This crisis will push all producers, including investor-led producers … towards automation and mechanization to a greater degree than they would have prior to the crisis" (Ali, 2020a). It is further reported that farm robotics and mechanization only accounted for US$179 million (1 per cent) of the total US$19.8 billion invested in ag-tech companies in 2019 (based on Agfunder data). Hence, investment in mechanization and automation had to be "ratcheted up significantly if it is truly set to solve the workforce issues exposed by the pandemic" (Ali, 2020a). The pandemic is thus presented as an important moment to be making this investment, supported by voices from within the industry: "Recession and covid is this perfect storm for advancing the field of robotics, from a customer interest standpoint, a decade forward" (Janiec, 2020c).

Lastly, food-tech investments are promoted as an important future growth sector. This growth is seen as driven not only by increasing consumer demand for alternatives to meat and dairy but also by major changes in how people are purchasing their food, where food is prepared, and how food is delivered to the consumer, as the entire food industry is going through a transformation. Here, an insider is quoted as saying, "Covid has accelerated changes to foodtech and to the supply chain. It has even affected how consumers eat, from curbside dining to takeout" (Goldfisher, 2020).

COVID-19 as a Push for Sustainability

A third theme is a stronger emphasis on sustainability, with the pandemic being presented as a "test" for future challenges in light of climate change. In this vein, a representative of McKinsey is quoted as saying, "Obviously, carbon management is not a global pandemic. They are quite different, but some of the ways companies have to respond have consistency to them ... If you believe post-covid we're all going to have some view of what needs to be done from a resilience standpoint, some of the challenges that climate change can raise tests our resilience in different forms" (Janiec, 2020a). Over the course of 2020, sustainability becomes an increasingly important theme in articles on the impact of, and lessons from, the pandemic. In an article titled "Sustainability now matters in PE", it is reported that British Private Equity and Venture Capital Association (BVCA) director general Michael Moore called the pandemic a reminder that the industry is both "an economic force and a social one". The article further states that the private equity ecosystem had come a long way in the past decade in terms of "accepting and integrating environmental, social and governance considerations into its investment processes". This was reflected in the inclusion of non-financial key performance indicators, such as carbon emissions (Mitchenall, 2020). Also, MIRA CEO O'Leary is portrayed as reflecting on the role that capital investment in agriculture could play "in making both societies and landscapes more resilient" (Kemp, 2020b). According to O'Leary, there is "strong proof" that sustainable farming addressing climate change is mutually beneficial to the environment and to the "farmer's bottom line". The way this is to be achieved is by increasing farmers' participation in sophisticated environmental markets, to "aid the decarbonization story" as well as more progressive farming practices adopted in an economically rational way (Kemp, 2020b).

Agriculture is, lastly, identified as playing a key role as the world moves towards greater resilience following COVID-19, notably in reducing emissions. Referring to a McKinsey representative, one article reports that agricultural companies were developing business models designed to benefit from potential future regulations on carbon emissions. The lack of large-scale carbon markets is seen as "limiting commitment among investors to finance emissions-reductions that do not present a clear return on investment" (Janiec, 2020a).

Cashing in on COVID-19?

COVID-19 has once again revealed the multiple flaws in our food system. That system is largely built on long-distance food supply chains, many of which have been disrupted due to lockdowns and trade restrictions. As food is treated not as a common good but as a commodity, people's food security depends on their purchasing power, which in many cases declined due to the pandemic-induced global recession. These vulnerabilities in the global food system, as Clapp and Moseley conclude, are neither new nor accidental. Rather, they are grounded in the policy responses to past food crises over 70 years that "have helped forge a global food system that is increasingly specialized, dependent on trade, and premised on the need to produce more food with industrial methods—all in the name of improving efficiency" (Clapp & Moseley, 2020, p. 1408). Yet, for some actors, crises also provide the opportunity for profit-making—a mechanism that Naomi Klein has famously termed "disaster capitalism", namely the implementation of calculated, free-market "solutions" to crises that exploit and exacerbate existing inequalities (Solis, 2020). Thus, as Reisman (2021, p. 911) observes, disaster moments such as the current pandemic require heightened caution about business activities "which momentarily suit crisis relief narratives but may ultimately serve other interests".

This chapter has investigated the responses of agri-food investors to the COVID-19 pandemic, demonstrating that agri-food investors used the most recent crisis to further strengthen the case for agri-investment, which—as the argument goes—has now proven itself not only lucrative but also a crisis-proof investment. While the 2007/2008 conjunction of events represented the "initial" crisis moment that incentivized investors to search for alternative investment possibilities, the pandemic has been presented as consolidating agriculture as an alternative investment class. The pandemic underlined the core fundamentals of the asset class—agri-food is not an outlier asset class any more but now qualifies as an "essential" sector. Can agri-food investment help to stabilize a pandemic- and increasingly crisis-ridden future food system, supporting its essential function for human survival? Or are agri-food investors' responses rather a form of "disaster capitalism"?

By way of conclusion, I make three observations. The first concerns the issue of "food security". The challenge to "feed the world" has been a consistent thread running through investor discourses associated with both crises and is used to morally legitimize and financially incentivize agri-food investment. Throughout both crises, however, the rhetoric followed a rather simplistic neo-Malthusian argument that "people need to eat" in moments of financial, economic or environmental crisis as much as they do during a pandemic. This narrative continuously disregards the complexity of food security and the well-established insight that food security is not only a matter of food being produced. As Sen (1981) famously formulated in his entitlement approach to food security, "it is fundamentally about who gets *access* to available food, which is about the distribution of wealth and resources" (Devereux et al., 2020, p. 771; emphasis added). The pandemic has not only affected food production and supply chains but also significantly lowered people's ability to access sufficient and nutritious food due to the consequences of lockdowns and economic recession, especially for vulnerable groups (Clapp & Moseley, 2020). Thus, financial investments that focus on food production and supply chains might allow investors to generate returns from an "essential sector"—but they do not help alleviate the food insecurity of those who cannot access food.

Second, the pandemic has been used to make the case for further investments in agriculture and food that go beyond those promoted in 2007/2008, most prominently investments in the recently much-hyped areas of ag- and food-tech. As Fairbairn and Guthman (2020, p. 587) note, Silicon Valley's ag- and food-tech scene was quick in identifying COVID-19 as an opportunity and presented the pandemic as amplifying the need for its existence (see also Reisman, 2021). As ag-investment in farming has become increasingly established, new digital ag- and food technologies are presented as a "fix" for social issues—such as exploitative labour conditions on farms and in processing factories—as well as under-capitalized and therefore newly emerging lucrative investment opportunities. Again, however, underlying issues of social inequalities and vulnerabilities of often migrant farm and food processing workers are not tackled within this approach but rather blatantly disregarded. Rather than suggesting that farm and factory workers' labour conditions need to change, the human factor is identified as the "problem" to discard.

Last, the pandemic has put sustainability and climate change much more prominently on the agenda, both of which were not part of the agri-food investor discourse in 2007/2008. As with the investment narratives outlined above, these issues are being addressed within a market and investment rationale, which suggests that more environmentally friendly and sustainable practices need to deliver returns to make them worthwhile considerations for investors. This argument is reminiscent of the ecological fix, which, as Bakker (2009, p. 1782, drawing on Vandana Shiva's description of "sustainable development") writes, is a means of "turning a potential threat into an opportunity". And even more so, within this discourse, we find the "threat" to not commit to, and implement, more sustainable practices if they are not presented as clear investment opportunities. While climate change and environmental issues are now at least recognized as important challenges facing the world, the agri-food investor discourse suggests that they are not tackled out of insight or necessity but only if the financial returns are worthwhile. In sum, while the agri-food investment discourse has moved on to new areas and issues due to the pandemic, its underlying logic has remained stable—amid calls for "more of the same" approaches to solve those crises it has helped to produce.

References

Ali, B. (2020a, July 8). Is the automation awakening afoot? *Agri Investor*. https://www.agriinvestor.com/is-the-automation-awakening-afoot/

Ali, B. (2020b, August 26). Four lessons coronavirus has taught us about ag. *Agri Investor*. https://www.agriinvestor.com/four-lessons-coronavirus-has-taught-us-about-ag/

Ali, B. (2020c, December 16). Ag looks to be on its way to a good 2021. *Agri Investor*. https://www.agriinvestor.com/ag-looks-to-be-on-its-way-to-a-good-2021/
Ali, B. (2021, January 15). In numbers: Agtech deals and fundraising to Q3 2020. *Agri Investor*. https://www.agriinvestor.com/in-numbers-agtech-deals-and-fundraising-to-q3-2020/
Bakker, K. (2009). Neoliberal nature, ecological fixes, and the pitfalls of comparative research. *Environment and Planning A, 41*(8), 1781–1787.
Bjørkhaug, H., Magnan, A., & Lawrence, G. A. (Eds.). (2018). *The financialization of agri-food systems: Contested transformations*. Routledge.
Clapp, J., & Cohen, M. J. (2009). The food crisis and global governance. In J. Clapp & M. J. Cohen (Eds.), *The global food crisis: Governance challenges and opportunities* (pp. 1–12). Wilfrid Laurier University Press.
Clapp, J., & Moseley, W. G. (2020). This food crisis is different: COVID-19 and the fragility of the neoliberal food security order. *The Journal of Peasant Studies, 47*(7), 1393–1417.
Corbett, M. (2020, December 21). Agriculture had a resilient 2020 and will have a solid 2021—Fiera Comox. *Agri Investor*. https://www.agriinvestor.com/agriculture-had-a-resilient-2020-and-will-have-a-solid-2021-fiera-comox/
Daniel, S. (2012). Situating private equity capital in the land grab debate. *The Journal of Peasant Studies, 39*(3–4), 703–729.
Devereux, S., Béné, C., & Hoddinott, J. (2020). Conceptualising COVID-19's impacts on household food security. *Food Security, 12*(4), 769–772.
Fairbairn, M. (2014). 'Like gold with yield': Evolving intersections between farmland and finance. *The Journal of Peasant Studies, 41*(5), 777–795.
Fairbairn, M. (2020). *Fields of gold: Financing the global land rush*. Cornell University Press.
Fairbairn, M., & Guthman, J. (2020). Agri-food tech discovers silver linings in the pandemic. *Agriculture and Human Values, 37*(3), 587–588.
Gertel, J., & Sippel, S. R. (2016). The financialisation of agriculture and food. In M. Shucksmith & D. L. Brown (Eds.), *International handbook of rural studies* (pp. 215–226). Routledge.
Goldfisher, A. (2020, October 9). Foodtech investing surges, accelerated by the coronavirus. *Agri Investor*. https://www.agriinvestor.com/foodtech-investing-surges-accelerated-by-the-coronavirus/
Janiec, C. (2020a, June 15). McKinsey sees momentum behind ag emissions reduction. *Agri Investor*. https://www.agriinvestor.com/mckinsey-sees-momentum-behind-ag-emissions-reduction/
Janiec, C. (2020b, August 3). AGR targets up to $300m for third fund—exclusive. *Agri Investor*. https://www.agriinvestor.com/agr-targets-up-to-300m-for-third-fund-exclusive/

Janiec, C. (2020c, September 1). Coronavirus has created "perfect storm" for ag robotics to thrive—Root, *AI*. https://www.agriinvestor.com/coronavirus-has-created-perfect-storm-for-ag-robotics-to-thrive-root-ai/

Janiec, C. (2021, February 1). State-owned investors now covet agtech more than farmland—Global SWF. *Agri Investor*. https://www.agriinvestor.com/state-owned-investors-now-covet-agtech-more-than-farmland-swf-global/

Kemp, D. (2020a, March 4). Coronavirus plays on the mind of agri investors worldwide. *Agri Investor*. https://www.agriinvestor.com/coronavirus-plays-on-the-mind-of-agri-investors-worldwide/

Kemp, D. (2020b, June 29). MIRA's Liz O'Leary on ag investments in the wake of coronavirus—exclusive interview. *Agri Investor*. https://www.agri-investor.com/miras-liz-oleary-on-ag-investments-in-the-wake-of-coronavirus-exclusive-interview/

Kemp, D. (2020c, December 24). Year of turmoil proves resilience of agriculture assets. *Agri Investor*. https://www.agriinvestor.com/year-of-turmoil-proves-resilience-of-agriculture-assets/

Kemp, D. (2020d, July 6). Kilter Rural's Ingram on fundraising challenges and ag's coronavirus resilience—interview. *Agri Investor*. https://www.agriinvestor.com/kilter-rurals-ingram-on-fundraising-challenges-and-ags-coronavirus-resilience-interview/

Larder, N., Sippel, S. R., & Lawrence, G. (2015). Finance capital, food security narratives and Australian agricultural land. *Journal of Agrarian Change, 15*(4), 592–603.

McMichael, P. (2014). Historicizing food sovereignty. *The Journal of Peasant Studies, 41*(6), 933–957.

McMichael, P., & Schneider, M. (2011). Food security politics and the Millennium Development Goals. *Third World Quarterly, 32*(1), 119–139.

Mitchenall, T. (2020, October 14). Covid-19 heralds hard decisions on sustainable investment. *Agri Investor*. https://www.agriinvestor.com/covid-19-heralds-hard-decisions-on-sustainable-investment/

Mittal, A. (2009). *The 2008 food price crisis: Rethinking food security policies*. UNCTAD G-24 Discussion Paper Series, No. 56, United Nations, New York, Geneva.

Reisman, E. (2021). Sanitizing agri-food tech: COVID-19 and the politics of expectation. *The Journal of Peasant Studies, 48*(5), 910–933.

Rosin, C. J., Stock, P. V., & Campbell, H. (2012). Introduction: Shocking the global food system. In C. J. Rosin, P. V. Stock, & H. Campbell (Eds.), *Food systems failure. The Global food crisis and the future of agriculture* (pp. 1–14). Routledge.

Sen, A. (1981). *Poverty and famines*. Oxford University Press.

Solis, M. (2020, March 13). Coronavirus is the perfect disaster for 'disaster capitalism': Naomi Klein explains how governments and the global elite will exploit a pandemic. *Vice News*. https://www.vice.com/en_us/article/5dmqyk/naomi-klein-interview-on-coronavirus-and-disaster-capitalism-shock-doctrine
Szkutak, R. (2020, November 24). Agtech offers room for a multitude of investors to take root. *Agri Investor*. https://www.agriinvestor.com/agtech-offers-room-for-a-multitude-of-investors-to-take-root/

PART II

Production

CHAPTER 4

Putting the Crisis to Work

Victoria Stead and Kirstie Petrou

Abstract As international borders closed amid the COVID-19 pandemic, the Australian horticultural industry experienced a dramatic reduction of key groups of workers upon which it has come to depend, particularly at harvest. These labour shortages focused public attention on the importance of seasonal labour for horticultural production and the availability of fresh fruit and produce, resulting in a paradoxical revaluation of that work. On the one hand, seasonal farm work was revalued as essential labour, and migrant workers were acknowledged as critical to Australia's food security. On the other hand, the increased visibility of seasonal farm work highlighted its systematic *de*valuing as so-called unskilled work that is done for low wages, under often poor conditions, and that is widely figured through racialized narratives. Faced with the prospect of critical labour shortages, both industry and government sought—and largely failed—to reinscribe the terms by which seasonal labour was imagined in attempts to make it attractive to "local" workers. What resulted was an entrenching of uneven distributions of precarity, risk and vulnerability along the fault lines of race and migration status.

V. Stead (✉) • K. Petrou
Alfred Deakin Institute for Citizenship and Globalisation, Deakin University, Burwood, VIC, Australia
e-mail: victoria.stead@deakin.edu.au; kirstie.petrou@deakin.edu.au

V. Stead, M. Hinkson (eds.), *Beyond Global Food Supply Chains*,
https://doi.org/10.1007/978-981-19-3155-0_4

Keywords Seasonal Worker Programme • Pacific Islander • Labour • Temporary migrants • Farmworkers • COVID-19

Introduction

Over recent decades, the Australian horticultural industry has come to depend, as have many global horticultural industries, on labour performed by highly mobile, seasonal workforces. Notwithstanding periodic media exposés of poor working conditions, the mobility and labour of this essential workforce—predominantly made up of non-white temporary migrants and concentrated in rural locations—have gone largely unremarked upon, and remained invisible to, the Australian citizenry. In March 2020, however, as borders snapped shut following the COVID-19 outbreak, horticultural labour issues were thrust into the public and political spotlight. International border closures saw Australia's overall horticultural workforce plummet as many temporary migrant workers—including those on Working Holiday Maker (WHM) visas, international students and Pacific Islanders employed through the Seasonal Worker Programme (SWP) guest worker scheme—returned home and replacements were unable to arrive. The heightened visibility of seasonal labour issues resulting from these shortages produced a paradoxical revaluing of this work. On the one hand, there was a renewed valuing of seasonal farm work as "essential" labour and of migrant workers as critical to Australia's food security—an awareness heightened by consumer experiences of empty shelves and stock shortages at the supermarket end of supply chains. Yet, the increased visibility of seasonal farm work also highlighted its systematic *de*valuing as "un-skilled" work that is done for low wages, often under poor conditions, and that, critically, is widely deemed unsuitable and unwanted by "local" workers. Attempts by industry and government to reinscribe the terms in which seasonal labour was imagined to make it attractive to local workers overwhelmingly failed. Nor did the recognition of seasonal labour as "essential" ultimately translate into increased economic valuation through significantly improved wages or conditions. Rather, what was demonstrated throughout the pandemic was the reassertion of structures and systems that unevenly distribute precarity, risk and vulnerability along the fault lines of race and migration status.

The shifting valuations of horticultural labour amid the pandemic highlight ambiguities inherent to value itself. In one sense, the simultaneous valuing and devaluing of seasonal labour is reflective of a tension running through all relations of capitalist production, as Marx theorized in his labour theory of value. That is, labour creates value (in the things it produces) in excess of the valuation of that labour through wages. In this sense, labour's valuation through wages *never* matches the value produced by labour, and it is this gap that produces profit for those controlling the means of production. In another sense, seasonal labour's simultaneous valuing and devaluing reflects an underlying ambiguity within which, as Graeber (2001) observes, value denotes at once the price of things (its economic sense), the extent to which a thing is considered desirable or good (its sociological sense) and the meaningful difference attributed to signifiers (its linguistic sense). The economic and sociological dimensions of value, particularly, converge in the figuring of horticultural labour through the pandemic, including through narratives that position it as work good for, and suited to, the bodies of migrants and others outside of the "citizenship-labour nexus" (Neilson & Rossiter, 2008, p. 59), even as political effort has also been put towards reactivating that nexus through appeals for local labour. These multiple dimensions of labour value reflect what others (e.g. Peck, 1996) have shown, namely that labour power is produced and reproduced through social as well as economic processes that extend beyond the workplace. These include migration regimes and strictures, which do not simply increase the total pool of available labour for industry but more specifically increase the availability of labour that is more exploitable and more suitable for subordination (Scott, 2013). They include racialized imaginaries and hierarchies that are themselves rooted in the histories and geographies of Empire (Stead, 2019, 2021).

Critical theorists of supply chains have highlighted the role of racialized, gendered, geographic and other forms of difference in their operation and in capitalist value creation (Bear et al., 2015; Tsing, 2009, 2016). In Anna Tsing's theorization of "supply chain capitalism", these form the basis of the kinds of "niche difference" (2009, p. 167) around which the different stages of geographically dispersed supply chains are organized. Diversity, for Tsing, is thus inherently bound up with *outsourcing* as a key technique of supply-chain capitalism, not as a peripheral consideration but as an integral part of its structure. Yet while Tsing's attention to the role of racialized relations in the organization of contemporary capitalist production resonates with the analysis we develop here, the kinds of horticultural production we are concerned with also differ in significant ways from models of global supply chains organized through outsourcing. Rather, the industry's use of temporary migrant labour provides what geographer Sam Scott (2013), writing about the UK fruit industry, has described, following Harvey, as an "*in situ* spatial fix". In the Australian context, this enables the reproduction of imaginatively charged narratives of national self-sufficiency that belie the kinds of dependencies, vulnerabilities and racialized inequalities laid bare by the pandemic.

In this chapter, we consider, first, the ways in which border logics and narratives of national self-sufficiency were mobilized in the early days of the pandemic. We then consider the widespread labour shortages and the awareness these generated about the industry's reliance on migration. We document both the various attempts to mobilize "local workers" and the narratives that framed these efforts and their failures. The gap between the narrative of self-sufficiency and the reliance on migrant workers is reflective, we argue, of ambiguities in how the scope and place of supply chains are conceptualized. The competing, sometimes contradictory imaginings of both local and migrant workers, meanwhile, speak to the shifting ways in which value is imagined, produced and assessed within these chains. In the final section, we focus on the operation of race, migration and visa status in the production of horticultural labour power and value.

Border Logics and Narratives of National Self-Sufficiency

Around the world, the COVID-19 pandemic prompted border closures and an amplification of border logics. On 19 March, eight days after the World Health Organization declared a global pandemic, Australian Prime Minister Scott Morrison announced international travel bans. With limited exemptions, only Australian citizens, permanent residents and their immediate family members were allowed to enter the country. At the same time, non-citizens within the country who were deemed not to be economically valuable were encouraged to leave. Speaking on 3 April, Morrison declared that people in Australia holding temporary visas and without the capacity to support themselves financially—including the tens of thousands whose casual jobs had been abruptly terminated due to the effects of lockdowns—should "return to their home countries" (Gibson & Moran, 2020). Australia, Morrison continued, needed to focus on its citizens and residents: "As much as it's lovely to have visitors to Australia in good times, at times like this, if you are a visitor in this country, it is time … to make your way home." The exception was those migrants, like "nurses or doctors", whose "critical skills" could assist in Australia's response to the crisis.

In this early, concentrated period of crisis response we see something of a reassertion of the "citizen-worker" as a political subject, a subjectivity previously theorized as in decline in the context of a globalizing economy and a polity marked by the prevalence of, and reliance on, migrant labour (Neilson & Rossiter, 2008). Here rights, protections, home and work itself are the domains of citizens. The exemption for "nurses or doctors" denotes both the exception amplifying the rule and assumptions of value tied to understandings of skill. These are themselves resonant with a longer-established Australian migration imaginary that has historically devalued "unskilled" and temporary migration, which have nevertheless become more prominent over recent decades, and on which many industries (like horticulture) now depend.

Alongside the closing of borders and calls for migrants to "go home", these early weeks of the pandemic also saw widespread panic-buying prompted by a series of city- and state-wide lockdowns. Resulting shortages of many staple items were further exacerbated by disruptions to logistics systems, with the unfamiliar spectre of empty supermarket shelves bringing the vulnerabilities of just-in-time food supply chains into public consciousness. The federal government responded to public concerns over struggling supply chains with forceful assertions of Australia's self-sufficiency in food production. Agriculture Minister David Littleproud slammed "ridiculous" panic-buying, writing, "It is important to understand that Australian farmers produce enough food for 75 million people: three times what we need." Farmers, he continued, are "calmly going about the business of food production" (Littleproud, 2020). By April, the government had produced a report emphasizing that empty shelves were merely a temporary "disruption" rather than an indication of food shortages. The report stressed that imports account for only 11 per cent of foods consumed in Australia and are "motivated by taste and variety" rather than a need to supplement local supplies (ABARES, 2020, p. 2). Despite the empty shelves, Australia's self-sufficiency was claimed to be assured.

"I Can't Get Workers"

Farmers were, however, far from "calm". The reliance of the horticultural industry on migrant labour is something that growers are keenly aware of, in ways that often run counter to the narratives of the predominantly urban-based political elite. Around 65,000 workers (out of a total industry workforce of 80,000) are employed annually to provide seasonal labour, including harvesting, picking, packing, planting and pruning (Australian Fresh Produce Alliance, n.d.). This work is almost invariably casual and paid by piece rates. Prior to the pandemic, only 5000 of these 65,000 workers were reported to be Australian citizens or permanent residents (although these figures, sourced from the Australian Bureau of Statistics, do not include the locally resident undocumented workers upon whose labour the industry is heavily reliant). Around 8000 were Pacific Islander temporary labour migrants employed through the SWP; 52,000 were other temporary migrants, mostly on WHM visas, including many European backpackers undertaking eighty-eight days of agricultural work in order to secure a second-year visa extension under the provisions of the WHM scheme. As migrant arrivals all but ceased, it quickly became clear that Australian growers would struggle to meet their peak seasonal labour requirements. In September 2020, Ernst & Young (2020) forecast a shortfall of 26,000 workers for the coming harvest.

Several months into the pandemic, stories about farming labour shortages, and their effects, were proliferating in the mainstream media. These stories tended to invoke motifs, well established within Australian rural imaginaries, of family farms and struggling "Aussie battlers". Vegetable growers in the Lindenow Valley were reported to have destroyed a celery crop worth $150,000 due to a lack of workers to pick it (Somerville et al., 2021). Salad grower Dino Boratto was described as having been forced to destroy $20,000 worth of spinach when he could not make up for the lost labour of fifteen "skilled" SWP workers. Boratto was quoted as describing how the major supermarkets had predicted a rise in demand for salad leaves over the Christmas season, a demand he could not meet without (migrant) labour: "I looked them in the face and said, 'Yeah? What do you want me to do? I can't get workers'" (Topsfield, 2020).

Locating Production

The divergences between government narratives of self-sufficiency, and industry highlighting its reliance on migrant workers, speak to ambiguity in how—and *where*—horticultural production is conceptualized. Supply-chain thinking invokes a fundamental linearity, with bracketed, end-to-end sequences of production stages across which value production is understood to be distributed (Lepawsky & Billah, 2011, p. 135). Where these chains extend across transnational space, this is understood to be the result of outsourcing (Tsing, 2009, 2016). In important respects, however, the landedness of farming proves resistant to geographical dispersion in horticultural production. The immobile materialities of trees and roots cannot be outsourced, even if supermarkets and buyers at the powerful consumer ends of food supply chains readily cast a global net in selecting from whom they buy. It is this sense of place-bound production—and the nationalistic and settler-colonial imaginaries bound up with it—that underpins the narratives of Australian self-sufficiency, as against government appeals for endless growth in agricultural export markets.

Labour shortages catalysed by the pandemic reveal the fault lines in this figuring. Horticultural supply chains, so imagined, might indeed fall within a national frame, but the industry's reliance on temporary migrant labour speaks to transnational aspects of production that fall outside the parameters of supply-chain modelling. In his analysis of the UK food industry, geographer Sam Scott (2013) draws on David Harvey's concept of the "spatial fix" to describe this use of migrant labour as an *in situ* spatial fix for capital, in contrast to the kinds of geographic expansion that Harvey's term is more often deployed to describe (cf. Anderson & Shuttleworth, 2004). Here, rather than stages of production being outsourced, what is shipped offshore is the work of producing the labour power that is then put to work in the fields and orchards into which workers are imported.

These slippages in geographic framing invite us to think not only about where supply chains begin and end—and the forces of production that exceed them—but also about the kinds of value through which supply chains themselves are produced. Doing so brings back to the fore the multiple and ambiguous ways in which value itself is conceived—the tensions between value as economic price and value as that which is deemed socially good (for particular groups of people). These paradoxes of value became acutely visible as both industry and government sought to mobilize local labour to fill the shortages created by the pandemic border closures.

Revaluing Local Labour?

As the scale and implications of seasonal labour shortages became clear, government and industry looked to entice local workers into horticulture. Some spruiked lucrative returns from the piece rates that have long been a point of contention between industry, government and unions. Agriculture Minister David Littleproud, for example, declared that workers in

Queensland were earning up to $3800 a week picking strawberries (labour that is widely documented, globally, as back-breakingly difficult and notoriously underpaid; see for example Holmes (2013) and Wells (1996)). Other proposed financial incentives included allowing workers to continue to receive JobSeeker (social security) payments while undertaking horticultural employment and one-off relocation payments to entice workers to rural locations facing labour shortages. The Northern Territory Farmers Association (NTFA), among others, suggested encouraging students to work in horticulture, promoting it as an alternative "gap year" option. Incentives such as reductions in tertiary student debt were considered, and NTFA chief executive Paul Burke suggested that a year working in rural and regional Australia could provide students with a valuable cultural exchange (Brann, 2020). Deputy Prime Minister Michael McCormack tried to lure young workers with promises of love and "Instagrammable" moments:

> If you know somebody who might be on the coast who might be lounging around with a surfboard, tell them to come to the regions ... Tell them to bring their mobile with them, because it would be a great Instagram moment for them ... who knows ... they might meet the love of their life. (Gillespie, 2020)

Di West, a strawberry grower from Queensland, issued a call to arms, asking Australians to "pick for their country". "You're just here for a brief time," she implored. "We need you to get out there and have a go and be a real Australian" (Nichols, 2020).

Even as unemployment rates rocketed upwards, these promises of love, money, national pride and Insta-fame fell flat. By 31 March 2021, only 871 people had received relocation assistance for working in horticulture (McGlone, 2021), while media reporting highlighted the material and economic realities of seasonal labour. A report on the New South Wales blueberry industry, based on data collected during the 2019/2020 season and released as industry and government representatives were heralding lucrative returns from piece rates, confirmed the prevalence of wage theft and exploitative conditions, with rates of pay documented as low as $3 per hour (Cavanough & Wherrett, 2020). Other reportage highlighted the experiences of the relative few who did respond to the "call to arms". Some accounts were broadly positive, if lacklustre in their enthusiasm. Eighteen-year-old Xavier Jackson, who was unemployed before working on a strawberry farm, said of the work, "It was a little tiring the first few days but I'm getting into it now and it's not as bad as I thought it'd be" (Nichols, 2020). Other reports were significantly more dire. One worker, who was paid for six ten-hour working days, described things ending "sourly" when he saw he had earned far less than expected. Another worker on the same farm, who had been enticed by the promise of "adventure", described feeling "a little bit taken advantage of" when he discovered that the piece rate he was paid did not even cover his accommodation costs (Uibu, 2021).

Union responses to both the call for local labour and the persistent labour shortages mirrored these critiques. There would be a "willing workforce already out there", suggested the Australian Workers Union, if farmers simply "started paying people decent wages" (Sullivan, 2020). In this gap between promise and reality, though, lies more than the question of decent wages. Encapsulated within both the calls to work and the ultimate failure to meet shortages with local labour are forms of valuation that extend far beyond issues of price, encompassing questions of goodness, desirability and suitability. It is to these questions of value, and the geographies and often racialized imaginaries that underpin them, that we turn in the final section.

Good Work, Good Workers?

If, as the union movement has emphasized, job insecurity and low rates of pay have proved disincentives for local workers to take up rural horticultural labour throughout the pandemic, the fact that this work was nevertheless readily filled with migrant workers prior to COVID-19—and the implications of this—should not be treated as self-evident. In his theorizing of the *in situ* spatial fix in the UK fruit industry, Scott (2013) suggests that the fix works for capital in two ways. First, it generates workers with forms of "human capital" desirable for industry, particularly migrant workers who are skilled and motivated (including because of economic necessity and the precariousness of their lives and visa statuses) to work in ways the industry finds productive. Second, it works to divide and discipline workers and limit opportunities for collective action, including in a context of neoliberal restructuring. Contingent visa statuses, North–South structural inequalities, and the absence of alternative welfare entitlements compel migrant labour power in ways that are less effective for citizen-workers. The distribution of "good" and "bad" workers, Scott observes, has a distinct geography.

In late 2020, a political decision was made to restart the intake of SWP workers under controlled conditions. Farmers' responses to this decision reflect these valuations of "good" migrant labour. Speaking to the media, mango farmer Barry Albrecht explained: "It costs us to bring them [SWP workers] in, with quarantine fees and all that. But we feel they're worth it … They're so easy to get along with: polite, well-mannered, clean" (Srinivasan, 2020). The flipside of these valuations was the admonishment of local workers by growers as lazy and work-shy. Thus, media coverage of pandemic labour shortages included accounts of willing Australians denied work by growers. One applicant, Lukus, reported:

> I've been told from a couple they're worried that, as an Australian, I'm going to be lazy … I'm not as exploitable as a foreigner … Now they're talking about fast-tracking Pacific Islander workers and that's fine, and all power to them, but if they won't even consider an Australian employee who's willing to work, then it leaves some questions. (Kelly, 2020)

The kinds of difference being mobilized here are not exclusively organized around visa and citizenship status. Throughout the industry, the descriptors "Australian" and "local" are widely used to denote white workers, as distinct from locally resident but non-white workers, such as settled Pacific Islander populations, asylum seekers or refugees, who are nonetheless excluded from the kinds of belonging that the descriptor "local" bestows, even if they are nominally considered harder-working or more desirable workers (Stead, 2019; Stead et al., 2022). These are, then, strongly racialized figurings of "insider" and "outsider". The exceptions are European backpackers, who form a large proportion of WHMs. It is notable, though, that the horticultural labour of these white workers is figured as temporary, just as it is imagined it might be for young "Aussies" who might take a pandemic fruit-picking "gap year"—an adventure good for an Instagram moment, but not the norm within the context of their lives and the social and cultural conditions of their making.

The valuations—in the broader sociological sense—of horticultural workers are thus deeply ambiguous. Local (white, often urban) workers are both the subject of nationalistic calls to arms and to adventure and admonished for their failure to live up to the imagined (rural) work ethic invoked by that nationalism. Migrant (often non-white) workers are valorized as good workers and the industry's "saviours", well-suited to work for which they nevertheless continue to receive poor pay and conditions.

Indeed, while proposals for enticing locals into the horticultural workforce involved financial incentives, the increased visibility and valuation of seasonal work as essential labour has not resulted in improved pay or conditions for the migrant and non-white resident workers who have remained the industry's mainstay. The experiences of those SWP workers who were already present in the country when the international borders were closed and who remained in Australia to continue working reflect this. The pandemic has intensified and extended existing issues in the SWP scheme, including isolation, restricted movement and inadequate pay (Petrou et al., 2021). Migrant workers have endured the stress of extended separation from their families, and some SWP employers have not allowed workers to return home when they wanted to. Increasingly, SWP workers have absconded from their places of employment due to insufficient work, meaning they will never be able to participate in the scheme again. Similarly entrenched conditions, and heightened vulnerabilities through the pandemic, have been documented globally (e.g. Haley et al., 2020; Neef, 2020).

Conclusion

If crisis is an idiom that works to stabilize existing structures, and to conceal the contradictions entrenched in twenty-first-century capitalism (Masco, 2017; Roitman, 2014), how was that idiom put to work in the context of horticultural labour relations during the pandemic? The crises projected through government, industry and public discourses included the material experiences of labour shortages and panic buying, but also the affective intensities of a white work ethic understood to be in decline and a mode of landedness (the family farm) experienced as under threat. In none of this, though, was attention focused on the conditions of possibility underpinning those experiences of crisis. By these, we do not mean the pandemic itself but rather the deeper-seated fault lines that the pandemic exposed—the inequalities and geographies of racialized capitalism, the colonial dispossessions out of which the Australian family farm is forged, the exclusions of border regimes, or the alienation of most people from the activity of food production and the role of powerful corporate agents in setting the terms of that alienation.

Rather, the pandemic labour shortages and empty supermarket shelves were recast as technical crises—that is, supply-chain problems—bracketed just as supply chains themselves are bracketed. In this vein, the pandemic's disruptions produced a renewed appreciation of seasonal labour as "essential" work, but left unchanged the economic terms and conditions of its valuation. Attempts to shift the industry's reliance on migrant workers through enticing a local workforce were, ultimately, cast as temporary measures—short-term and extraordinary responses to labour shortages imagined as temporary interruptions to production systems otherwise figured by capital as smooth, efficient, just-in-time and not in need of transformation.

References

ABARES. (2020). *Analysis of Australian Food Security and the COVID-19 Pandemic*. Department of Agriculture, Water and the Environment, Canberra. Retrieved November 20, 2020, from https://www.agriculture.gov.au/abares/products/insights/australian-food-security-and-COVID-19

Anderson, J., & Shuttleworth, I. (2004). *Theorizing state borders in capitalism: Spatial fixes old and new*. Centre for International Borders Research.

Australian Fresh Produce Alliance. (n.d.). Who does the industry employ? Retrieved May 15, 2021, from http://freshproduce.org.au/workforce-shortages/industryemployment/

Bear, L., Ho, K., Tsing, A. L., & Yanagisako, S. (2015, March 30). Gens: A feminist manifesto for the study of capitalism. *Fieldsights*. Retrieved June 02, 2021, from https://culanth.org/fieldsights/gens-a-feminist-manifesto-for-the-study-of-capitalism

Brann, M. (2020, September 10). Give HECS discount to university students willing to pick fruit, says NT Farmers Association. *ABC News*. Retrieved November 20, 2020, from https://www.abc.net.au/news/rural/2020-09-10/farm-labour-shortage-hecs-subsidy-for-students-to-pick-fruit/12641778

Cavanough, E., & Wherrett, C. (2020). *Blue harvest: Wage theft and other labour infringements in the NSW Mid-north coast's 2019/20 Berry Harvest*. The McKell Institute.

Ernst & Young. (2020). *Seasonal horticulture labour demand and workforce study*. Hort Innovation. Retrieved May 23, 2021, from https://www.horticulture.com.au/growers/help-your-business-grow/research-reports-publications-fact-sheets-and-more/st19040/

Gibson, J., & Moran, A. (2020, April 3). As coronavirus spreads, "it's time to go home" Scott Morrison tells visitors and international students. *ABC News*. Retrieved

November 20, 2020, from https://www.abc.net.au/news/2020-04-03/coronavirus-pm-tells-international-students-time-to-go-to-home/12119568

Gillespie, E. (2020, 30 September). 'Do it for the gram': Deputy PM tells young Aussies to work as fruit pickers for the Instagram opportunities. *SBS: The Feed*. Retrieved October 14, 2020, from https://www.sbs.com.au/news/the-feed/do-it-for-the-gram-deputy-pm-tells-young-aussies-to-work-as-fruit-pickers-for-the-instagram-opportunities

Graeber, D. (2001). *Toward an anthropological theory of value: The false coin of our own dreams*. Palgrave.

Haley, E., Caxaj, S., George, G., Hennebry, J. L., Martell, E., & McLaughlin, J. (2020). Migrant farmworkers face heightened vulnerabilities during COVID-19. *Journal of Agriculture, Food Systems, and Community Development, 9*(3), 35–39.

Holmes, S. (2013). *Fresh fruit, broken bodies: Migrant farmworkers in the United States*. University of California Press.

Kelly, C. (2020, October 25). 'I'm not as exploitable as a foreigner': Lukus is young and fit, but no farm will give him a go. *The New Daily*. Retrieved November 20, 2020, from https://thenewdaily.com.au/news/national/2020/10/25/farm-jobs-shortage-australia/

Lepawsky, J., & Billah, M. (2011). Making chains that (un)make things: Waste-value relations and the Bangladesh rubbish electronics industry. *Geografiska Annaler: Series B, Human Geography, 93*(2), 121–139.

Littleproud, D. 2020. Don't panic, Australia. The coronavirus doesn't mean we'll run out of food. *The Guardian*, March 19.

Masco, J. (2017). The crisis in crisis. *Current Anthropology, 58*, S65–S76.

McGlone, T. (2021, April 11). Seasonal work on Australia's farms: "No one wants to do this sort of work". *The Guardian*.

Neef, A. (2020). Legal and social protection for migrant farm workers: Lessons from COVID-19. *Agriculture and Human Values, 37*, 641–642.

Neilson, B., & Rossiter, N. (2008). Precarity as political concept, or, Fordism as exception. *Theory, Culture & Society, 25*(7–8), 51–72.

Nichols, J. (2020, September 7). Australians urged to backpack in their own backyards and stop fruit going to rot. *ABC News*. Retrieved November 20, 2020, from https://www.abc.net.au/news/rural/2020-09-07/backpack-in-your-own-backyard-to-pick-fruit/12635890?fbclid=IwAR3VH-PC3ksNK732QvdlJ90H3Vr9fL-hXLNun61pZz1fd6MF1Ab1GQ46q5s

Peck, J. (1996). *Workplace: The social regulation of labour markets*. Guilford Press.

Petrou, K., Dun, O., Farbotko, C., & Kitara, T. (2021). Pacific Labour Mobility on pause: the consequences of temporary immobility during the COVID-19 pandemic. In *COVID in the Islands: A comparative perspective on the Caribbean and the Pacific Y. Campbell and J. Connell, eds.* (pp. 299–319) Palgrave Macmillan.

Roitman, J. (2014). *Anti-crisis*. Duke University Press.

Scott, S. (2013). Migration and the spatial fix: Evidence from the UK food industry. *Antipode, 45*(5), 1090–1109.
Somerville, P., McNaughton, J., & Lazzaro, K. (2021, January 13). Vegetable growers forced to dump $150,000 worth of celery crops due to picker shortage. *ABC News.* Retrieved May 27, 2021, from https://www.abc.net.au/news/rural/2021-01-14/veg-harvest-dumped-in-gippsland-due-to-covid-travel-bans/13056820
Srinivasan, P. (2020, September 27). After two weeks in hotel quarantine 162 seasonal workers from Vanuatu begin their work at Northern Territory mango farms. *ABC News.* Retrieved November 20, 2020, from https://www.abc.net.au/news/2020-09-27/vanuatu-men-and-women-australia-pick-fruit-coronavirus-pandemic/12699066
Stead, V. (2019). Money trees, development dreams and colonial legacies in contemporary Pasifika horticultural labour. In V. Stead & J. Altman (Eds.), *Labour lines and colonial power: Indigenous and pacific islander labour mobility in Australia* (pp. 133–157). ANU Press.
Stead, V. (2021). Precarity's reach: Intersections of history, life, and labour in the Australian horticultural industry. *Journal of the Royal Anthropological Institute, 27*, 303–320.
Stead, V., Taula, L., & Silaga, M. (2022). Making place in a place that doesn't recognise you: Racialised labour and intergenerational belonging in an Australian horticultural belonging. *Rural Studies.*
Sullivan, K. (2020, August 11). Unions want working holidaymaker visa axed, say pandemic shows farmers' over-reliance on backpackers. *ABC News.* Retrieved November 20, 2020, from https://www.abc.net.au/news/2020-08-11/unions-call-for-end-to-working-holidaymaker-visa/12542100
Topsfield, J. (2020, September 29). Destroying spinach and sacrificing cabbages: The worker drought wasting Australia's produce. *The Sydney Morning Herald.* Retrieved November 20, 2020, from https://www.smh.com.au/national/destroying-spinach-and-sacrificing-cabbages-the-worker-drought-wasting-australia-s-produce-20200929-p560es.html
Tsing, A. (2009). Supply chains and the human condition. *Rethinking Marxism, 21*(2), 148–176.
Tsing, A. (2016). What is emerging? Supply chains and the remaking of Asia. *The Professional Geographer, 68*(2), 330–337.
Uibu, K. (2021, January 14). When backpackers went home, these Australians gave farm jobs a go. Here's how they went. *ABC News.* Retrieved May 17, 2021, from https://www.abc.net.au/news/2021-01-14/when-backpackers-went-home-these-australians-tried-farm-work/1304706
Wells, M. (1996). *Strawberry fields: Politics, class, and work in California agriculture.* Cornell University Press.

CHAPTER 5

Going Against the Grain in the West Australian Wheatbelt

Kelly Donati

Abstract The vast wheatbelt of Western Australia marks a disruptive force on an ancient landscape, an upheaval wrought by the dispossessive ecologies of sheep and wheat (Mayes, *Unsettling Food Politics: Agriculture, Dispossession and Sovereignty*. London: Rowman & Littlefield, 2018). This chapter asks what transformational possibilities might emerge in this context through a case study of a broad-acre regenerative-farming couple, Di and Ian Haggerty, and their experiments with new ways of knowing, living and farming in the wheatbelt. The Haggertys seek to reconfigure ecological relations within regimes of large-scale production. On the one hand, these regimes of production look much like their neighbours', as they use the same logistical chains, infrastructure and financial systems as other wheatbelt producers. On the other, their farming practice—informed by a probiotic and more-than-human epistemology the Haggertys call "natural intelligence"—suggests a potential disruption to extractivist commodity agriculture in the wheatbelt and the hegemony of its technoscientific institutions. While regenerative farming at scale could be dismissed as a greener

K. Donati (✉)
Faculty of Higher Education, William Angliss Institute,
Melbourne, VIC, Australia
e-mail: Kelly.Donati@angliss.edu.au

V. Stead, M. Hinkson (eds.), *Beyond Global Food Supply Chains*,
https://doi.org/10.1007/978-981-19-3155-0_5

form of settler-colonial agriculture, this case study suggests, or at least creates space for, a cautious optimism that more diverse ways of knowing and doing food might be constructed from within the cracks of global supply chains and that new alliances might emerge from the ground up.

Keywords Wheatbelt • Australia • Regenerative agriculture • Epistemology • Multispecies studies

Introduction

The wheatbelt of Western Australia (WA) marks a disruptive force on an ancient landscape, an upheaval wrought by social and agricultural policies of the twentieth century that enrolled the dispossessive ecologies of sheep and wheat against the Noongar people and their country (Mayes, 2018). Tony Hughes-d'Aeth describes the wheatbelt's creation as nothing less than "a vast and almost total destruction of a pre-existing lifeworld"—so stark that it is visible from space (Hughes-d'Aeth, 2017, p. 3). Its fragile soils have been subject to relentless tillage and burning. Salt creeps slowly to the surface in the absence of deep-rooted vegetation, evoking a bleak sense of "life trying to die or death trying to live" (Hughes-d'Aeth, 2012, p. 26). These scars only hint at a profound and lasting trauma that is at once ecological, spiritual, social and cultural. This trauma, rooted in the settler-colonial logic of capitalist agriculture that exploits the earth and people as resources for endless extraction, is a historical fact and colonial present—sustained through structural imperatives and technoscientific imaginaries that mobilize farmers, economies, ecologies and knowledge systems in its service.

This chapter asks what transformational possibilities might emerge in this seemingly unpromising landscape. Exploring the grounded practices of a broad-acre farming couple and their experiments with new ways of knowing and farming in the wheatbelt, I argue for the possibility of a less anthropocentric agriculture to emerge from within the temporalities of global supply chains. While their farming practices are imbricated in the messy realities and destructive tendencies of contemporary capitalism, and thus enmeshed in contradictions and susceptible to co-optation, Di and Ian Haggerty's farming practice nevertheless suggests ways for resisting the hegemonic epistemologies of commodity agriculture and reveals something of the incomplete and "unstable commitments" of supply-chain capitalism (Tsing, 2009, p. 151). These instabilities of capitalism's "blasted landscapes" are consequential, for, as Anna Tsing cautions, "progress still controls us even in tales of ruination", and yet it is "not the only plan for making worlds" (Tsing, 2015, p. 21).

Regenerating at Scale

Di and Ian grew up on multi-generational farms in the wheatbelt but have worked together and separately in a range of agricultural businesses from the Kimberley to the southern reaches of Western Australia. In the early 1990s, they purchased a small parcel of degraded, inexpensive land next to Di's parents' farm. Cracks appeared in their own farming practices during the millennium drought, prompting a shift away from conventional agriculture. Today they seek to redress well-rehearsed fault lines of commodity agriculture: intensive chemical inputs, pesticide and herbicide resistance, declining soil fertility and crop nutrition, land desertification and salinization, diminished human health, biodiversity loss and climate change. The Haggertys, however, are motivated not by yield but by the regeneration of lifeworlds in the wheatbelt and beyond in ways that call into question the temporalities of "a productionist ethos that subjects soil care and … human–soil relations, to the extraction of future economic value" (Puig de la Bellacasa, 2015, p. 698).

The Haggertys are not necessarily striving to shorten supply chains or localize markets, though during the COVID crisis they began supplying a local miller and baker located 190 kilometres away in Perth. Their production system looks quite conventional—they use logistics infrastructure, agricultural machinery and financial systems similar to other wheatbelt producers. Their non-mulesed wool sells at a premium price in Europe, but their grain mostly enters undifferentiated global supply chains. The Haggertys' farming enterprise now spans 65,000 acres through purchasing or leasing adjoining farmland as it becomes available. Scale enables them to bring more people onto the farm and teach other ways of feeling and doing farming. As Ian explains: "you take some time and you explain … what you're looking at and what you're feeling [and] what they think, what they see". As such, farming at scale is a deliberate strategy to "build that community of connectedness with the Country". Ian adds: "If you haven't inherited [land], it's really hard to get the capital, but … there's lots of really good people out there that would love to get connected with the land and be farmers that haven't got a chance". Farming at scale also enables the Haggertys to observe and respond to how ecological processes such as water and nutrient cycling work across the landscape rather than on individual parcels of land. Newly acquired land, usually degraded and often saline, allows them to experiment across diverse conditions and soils.

Temporalities of Regeneration

Despite its popularity in alternative food and farming movements, regenerative agriculture resists definition, as revealed by a recent review of journal articles and practitioner websites (Newton et al., 2020). Scholar and regenerative farmer Charles Massy, whose 2017 book *Call of the Reed Warbler* has been influential in shaping the discourse surrounding regenerative agriculture in Australia, defines it as a mode of farming that enables landscapes to renew themselves. At the heart of "renewal" sit the epistemological dimensions of agriculture. Massy contrasts the "organic" or ecological mind of regenerative farming with the "mechanical mind" of Enlightenment thinking that "paved the way for the rise of Capitalism" and its handmaiden settler-colonial agriculture (Massy, 2017, p. 40). Maria Puig de la Bellacasa argues that the mechanistic epistemologies and technoscientific temporalities of productivism follow a "linear imperative of progress" but also a "restless futurity" that continually generates crisis and seeks out "hope for salvation" (2015, p. 694). In the face of the existential threat of climate change, Matthew Kearnes and Lauren Rickards observe how regenerative agriculture and its commitments to soil ecology and carbon sequestration are laden with a "promissory logic and … high hopes for a brighter future" (2020, p. 71).

Many scholars caution that the microbial turn in soil science, even within regenerative agriculture, is not inured to instrumentalist capture. Emerging scientific interests in soil life promise much for reimagining other soil futures yet "retain a productivist orientation" that risks commodifying biotic worlds (Granjou & Phillips, 2019, p. 412). Krzywoszynska is hopeful about the possibilities of a probiotic soil consciousness for more resilient futures but remains alert to how putting soil biota to work fails as a disruptive force if it replicates "the same processes of alienation and exploitation that characterize the relations between capital and human labor" (2020, p. 231). If regenerative agriculture merely harnesses microbial life as a new frontier of cheap labour for productivist accumulation, it simply remakes soil life as a commodity in existing "circuits of production and consumption" (Patel & Moore, 2018, p. 23). In this context, it is perhaps unsurprising that Nestlé, the world's largest food and drink conglomerate, is celebrating its investment in regenerative farming and its efforts at product reformulation to lower the carbon footprint of its processed foods (Nestlé, 2021). The revised narrative of progress promised by regenerative agriculture and circulating within global food regimes reveals an ecological modernism that upholds "the rationality of the market and the economic grammar of yield, consumer demand, ethical consumption, and neoliberal subjectivity" (Mikulak, 2013, p. 46).

Nonetheless, the processes of landscape renewal called for by Massy and the Haggertys operate according to a rhythm not easily subsumed into the input–output linearity of productivism, representing a fundamental "clash of temporalities" between understanding soil as a "slowly renewable entity" and putting it to work as an "accelerated technological solution" that preserves the futurity of productivist agriculture (Puig de la Bellacasa, 2015, p. 699). In her analysis of "soil care" among permaculture and biodynamic practitioners, Puig de la Bellacasa attends to how "care time … is irreducible to productionist time" and offers "an invitation to rearrange and rebalance the relations between a diversity of coexisting temporalities that inhabit the worlds of soil and other interdependent ecologies" (2015, pp 707–709). It is through this lens that I read the Haggertys' natural-intelligence system as a probiotic practice that feeds into undifferentiated global supply chains and concomitantly seeks to decentre technoscientific temporalities and cultivate webs of multispecies care across landscape functions and scales.

Natural Intelligence as Probiotic Governance

The Haggertys are recognized leaders in an emerging regenerative-farming movement that takes a keen interest in the entanglements of life-worlds. Their farming practices reflect a "probiotic governance" that Jamie Lorimer describes as "using life to manage life"; these are practices that seek to "transform the dynamics of the ecologies with which they are entangled, working from the bodies of animals out to the planetary concentration and circulation of atmospheric gases" and, in the process, diverge "markedly from the command-and-control logics of modern antibiotic approaches to human and environmental health" (2020, p. 7). The Haggertys' probiotic practices begin with sowing a diversity of cash crops—wheat, barley, oats, triticale, plus fodder crops—using a conventional no-till drill seeder that injects worm liquid and compost tea brewed on their farm directly into the soil. This microbially active liquid helps seedlings produce a thick rhizosheath that creates a complex root network before their leaves reach out for the sweetness of the sun. Growing deep into sandy soils and acidic subsoils, these roots improve soil structure and aeration while sequestering carbon from the plant's photosynthetic and respiratory metabolism. Even in low rainfall, they demonstrate remarkable capacity to source minerals, nutrients and water. Barley has proven particularly effective for rehabilitating saline soils. When a paddock is too saline even for barley, the Haggertys plant other salt-tolerant perennial shrubs and trees, providing habitat for insects and birds along with fodder for sheep. The re-emergence of native perennial grasses lying dormant in the soil signals that a paddock is regenerating.

The Haggertys attune themselves to dynamic ecologies circulating between the microbiomes of humans, sheep, soil and even the atmosphere in ways that exist within but also exceed the circuits of capital. Often regarded as a "dead, dormant, or inactive" dumping ground for carbon emissions, the atmosphere is "a habitat with actively reproducing microbial life", yet it is relatively neglected in regenerative-farming circles (Klein et al., 2016). Di has learned that the atmospheric microbiome comprises bacteria and bioaerosols that, among other things, help clouds to nucleate raindrops, thus attracting rain to an increasingly inhospitable wheatbelt.

The Haggertys nurture radical aspirations to create a substantial corridor of diversified tree plantings that would connect their farm to other large-scale replantings further south, having recently leased more land at the southernmost point on their farm. This ambition requires time, resources and a certain degree of luck in accessing adjacent properties before they are snatched up by land speculators. They aim to cultivate relations of care at individual, regional and planetary scales between terrestrial creatures in need of refuge, forested landscapes and the atmosphere's unknown microbial communities. This life web of multispecies care allows, Di explains, "all the soil microbes and the insects and the animals and so forth to have a refuge … when the season goes to shit and it doesn't rain for the right period of time". Over timescales that may exceed their own lives, the Haggertys imagine how trees might attract rain-making clouds and revitalize the microbial reciprocity of the soil biome, phytobiome and atmosphere. This attentiveness to multi-scalar, creaturely interconnectedness suggests, following Lorimer, how "managing microbiomes becomes a story of making kin across social and species difference" but also across temporalities (2020, p. 222).

Ovine Epistemology and Paddock Thinking

Where the Haggertys differ most from the broader regenerative-farming community is in their unconventional epistemic practices for acknowledging and responding to the more-than-human intelligence of sheep and even paddocks. Their natural-intelligence farming system developed through "hybrid epistemological work" that is informed by scientific literature in climate change, rumen health and soil biology, but also actively decentres mechanistic ways of knowing the world (Kearnes & Rickards, 2020, p. 83). Their unorthodox epistemic practices form an "unspoken discipline" that Ian admits they "don't normally talk about because it's not scientifically proven". The Haggertys have experienced how unorthodox thinking is sometimes denigrated or dismissed as "unscientific spiritual talk" within productivist circles (Puig de la Bellacasa, 2015, p. 708). Far from unscientific, they have developed nuanced epistemic practices for making sense of the land, each in their own way.

Di, who manages the livestock, sees ecological renewal as co-produced through the nested microbiomes of sheep rumen, soil and, she hopes, the humans who eat her food. Her sheep graze and browse on fodder crops, trees and brush planted across the paddocks along with supplements of hay. Ensuring there is native vegetation in every paddock enhances the farm's biodiversity and the dietary diversity of the flock. Sheep are the first step in a long process of soil rehabilitation, being fed the Haggertys' own hay to avoid disrupting rumen stability as sheep move between paddocks. Their manure helps spread microbes; their bodies carry and distribute native grass seed. By keeping a self-replacing flock, lambs are exposed *in utero* to the flavours and nutrients of the paddock; learning to eat alongside their mothers inoculates the lamb's undeveloped rumen microflora and cultivates an "intense knowledge" of their local environment, says Di. Over time, she has noticed sheep selecting from an increasing diversity of forage: "The animals seem to really blossom in their health, so that opened different thought patterns to us and just that interaction between their gut microbes and then into the soil was a lot better outcome". Observing the sheep informs Di's decisions about how to best support the intergenerational transfer of ovine ways of knowing, in turn further developing the epistemic capacities of her sheep.

Being with sheep helps Di enter into a meditative state that opens her mind to the paddock. It took Di years to quieten her rationalist mind and cultivate a more nuanced intention as she stands in the middle of a paddock that feeds into global supply chains. "Too much pressure makes it go hairy", she explains. "If you're looking from a personal perspective of greed or whatever else, it's going to go pear-shaped … It gives you more responsiveness to what's going on around you instead of just bulldozing your way through." She acknowledges that her financial stake in the land risks impeding her clarity in listening to what the paddock may reveal in that moment: "there's some decisions that you're making—and it is a big business at the end of the day—that you don't want your own personal bias to influence you. You want to try and be open … The mind can lead you down paths that might not necessarily be for the best". This "paddock thinking", as I call it, fosters an epistemological intersubjectivity that acknowledges the land and animals as knowing and challenges Di to resist productivist temporalities and decentre their anthropocentric imperatives.

Ian, who manages the cropping, understands how easy it is to disconnect from the paddock when riding an enormous, air-conditioned tractor for spraying compost tea or harvesting: "in a 24-hour period, you can cover a number of paddocks—big area—and you just roll them all into one. But they're all different". He makes a point of jumping out of the tractor at the end of a run to ensure he accounts for these differences: "you've got to make a physical, conscious effort to take time out and look at each paddock—each area as an individual—because it's too easy to bulk it all into one and think 'oh yeah, while we're doing that paddock, we'll just blooming do that one in the middle …' Two hours later, it's gone, and what you did is not right for it". Stepping out of the tractor allows Ian to note the paddock's relation to wind, whether its perennial grasses are still green, how recently they acquired the land and its state of vulnerability. Like Di, he consciously makes time to connect energetically with the land so it can guide how he proceeds: "I can hop on a machine, and I do one row of paddock and know this is just not right … [I] fold up and go and put it somewhere else because the paddock will basically just about tell you". Ian feels that a genuine commitment to "getting out of your own self" is critical for decision-making of this kind. Difficult to articulate through technoscientific rationalities, it partly hinges on a temporality that creates a space in which "plants can articulate and humans can listen to voices that function without language", albeit always imperfectly (Meldrum, 2009, p. 331). Treating each paddock as a distinct collective enables the Haggertys to farm at scale without compromising the intimate relationality needed for the paddock to reveal something about itself. This alternative temporal approach, Di explains, means that "the paddock can unfold on its own terms. They show their strengths better. Some are better as diverse grazing paddocks, and others do nicely with growing a crop".

The Haggertys' successes in regenerating land allow them to function within global supply chains. Yet earning a living from the land entails a delicate negotiation between the interests of the paddock and those of productivity. Yield is essential to the Haggertys' economic survival but forms only part of the story in how ecological worlds are remade. Ian explains, "Sure, we want to maximise our yield where we can, but you don't maximise your yield at the cost of the environment. So, the yield really is the last thing on the list". Other forms of accounting are needed to respond to the temporalities of a paddock's vulnerabilities and lively capacities. The Haggertys have learned that prioritizing yield by forcing a vulnerable paddock into production too early can cause a whole crop to be lost and add years to a paddock's recovery. In a "forced system", as Di describes it, chemical inputs compress time to extract higher yields. Natural-intelligence farming produces alternative temporal obligations: "you've got to work within the natural processes of that land, and it needs time. Sometimes it needs time just to rest, so it means it might not have a crop in it. It might not have animals on it. It might just be plants … sitting there if the seasonal conditions aren't conducive to growth at that particular time".

The epistemic practices and temporalities of paddock thinking were profoundly influenced by the years the Haggertys spent in remote communities of the Kimberley. As Ian explains, "They [Aboriginal Elders] were displaced from the landscape, but their knowledge of Country—and how they looked at Country and what they expected from Country—they didn't have high expectations of it … Those old fellows knew when it was going to rain, when it was going to be a good season, when it was going to be a bad season, what to do. Unless you're a totally arrogant prick, you sit back and take notice of it all. It did really shape ... what we're talking about: intuition, gut feeling, this connectedness". The Haggertys make no claims as holders or practitioners of Aboriginal knowledge, but their encounters with Elders did provoke a realization that other ways of knowing are possible, destabilizing the hegemonic authority of the technoscientific expertise they once relied upon. Through their hybrid epistemic practices, they have learned to demand less of the land yet, in other ways, to ask much more of it—not in terms of yield but in what the land can reveal about itself.

Regenerative Farming on Country

Regenerative farming at scale remains deeply imbricated within the global food system and yet, as the Haggertys' farming practices suggest, it needn't be subsumed within the temporalities of productivist agriculture. At the same time, not even the most ecologically benign agriculture can be prised from the colonial violence that reorganized webs of life across Australia. All agriculture—regenerative or otherwise—takes place on stolen lands. Regenerative agriculture cannot simply put Country, or *boodja* in Noongar language, to work in more ecological ways or be wielded as an epistemological tool for settler-colonial agriculture to think its way out of the mess of climate change. The push for ecological regeneration of the wheatbelt remains incommensurable with the Noongar pursuit of self-determination, land justice and spiritual healing (Tuck & Yang, 2012). Indigenous epistemologies have much to contribute to both regenerative agriculture and responses to the complexities of climate change, but Tony Birch cautions against Indigenous knowledge becoming "branded and packaged as a quick fix solution to climate change by retro-fitting it to suit Western society" (2017). However, Birch and others (Mayes, 2018) argue that growing concerns about climate change may also provide common ground and a shared agenda from which Indigenous communities and settler farmers might collaborate.

The Haggertys are clear that the project of healing Country through regenerative agriculture should not proceed without Noongar people. Di describes private land as an ownership model that operates according to false temporalities. "We're only here temporarily", she explains. "We need to look at different models of engagement of land and people." At the time of writing this chapter, she was in the early stages of exploring a possible collaboration with a Noongar enterprise to establish its own business on her farm utilizing bush foods and other native plants she has cultivated.

Other opportunities for collaboration are emerging. Justin Wolfgang, who works closely with the Haggertys through his advocacy of regenerative agriculture in WA, notes that the scale of landscape restoration that many regenerative farmers aspire to is hindered by the lack of tree nurseries to supply them. The Noongar Land Enterprise (NLE) recently purchased a nursery, now called Boola Boornap (The Place of Many Trees), which will raise tree seedlings endemic to south-west Western Australia. As NLE chairperson and Noongar business and community leader Oral McGuire explains at the public opening of the nursery, "many of our sacred trees and sacred places have been lost. So, the replenishment of trees into the spirit of the land is such an important part of the restoration and the ecological health of *boodja* ... we must do it with trees. Every tree that we grow is absolutely handled with the love and care of a baby" (Danjoo Koorliny, 2021). McGuire's vision is that every Noongar nation will have its own nursery where values of sacredness, spiritual and ecological renewal, love, and care will be made visible and given expression within the context of economic development. McGuire articulates a hybrid set of epistemological and economic practices that are underpinned by Noongar cultural law and intergenerational responsibility and that exist within but are not easily subsumed by the temporalities of capitalist imperatives. The nursery enterprise might draw on networks and markets of settler-colonial agriculture and yet remain uncompromisingly organized around the healing of *boodja*. If successful, this NLE model of economic development would enable Noongar people to work and live on Country while also contributing to large-scale ecological restoration.

Conclusion

Through their hybrid practice, the Haggertys negotiate a constant contradiction: while yield is not their primary motivation, it is a structural necessity if they wish to enact wide-scale ecological transformations. They will not "destroy the system" (Tsing, 2009), but their farming is consequential, particularly if it serves to undermine the hegemonic influence of agrochemical industries in the wheatbelt. The epistemic pluralism of natural-intelligence farming does not merely put the soil to work in new ways. In resisting the temporalities of technoscientific productivism, webs of life are reorganized and practices of care are attenuated across timescales and species difference in ways that allow other interests in the landscape to surface. This offers cause for cautious optimism for how the "possibilities for a more livable world" might emerge, as Tsing suggests, even from within the wheatbelt's most blasted landscapes (2009, p. 172). It might also suggest how regenerative agriculture could support an alternative hybrid economy that "valu[es] Aboriginal work and country" in ways that reflect the aspirations and imaginaries of the Noongar community (Altman, 2012, p. 21). The disruptive potential for collaborations in the wheatbelt ultimately rests on the extent to which sovereignty is acknowledged, settler epistemologies are decentred and, critically, Noongar strategies to work and live on Country are supported. As runaway climate change bears down on all life, these collaborations could carve out the space from which a truly counterhegemonic practice of regenerative agriculture might emerge in Australia.

References

Altman, J. (2012). People on country as alternate development. In J. Altman & S. Kerins (Eds.), *People on country: Vital landscapes, Indigenous futures* (pp. 1–22). Federation Press.

Puig de la Bellacasa, M. (2015). Making time for soil: Technoscientific futurity and the pace of care. *Social Studies of Science, 45*(5), 691–716.

Birch, T. (2017). Climate change, recognition and social place-making. *Sydney Review of Books*, March 3. Retrieved August 15, 2021. https://sydneyreviewofbooks.com/essay/climate-change-recognition-and-caring-for-country/

Granjou, C., & Phillips, C. (2019). Living and labouring soils: Metagenomic ecology and a new agricultural revolution? *BioSocieties, 14*(3), 393–415.

Hughes-d'Aeth, T. (2012). Salt scars: John Kinsella's Wheatbelt. *Australian Literary Studies, 27*(2), 18–31.

Hughes-d'Aeth, T. (2017). *Like nothing on this earth: A literary history of the Wheatbelt*. UWA Publishing.

Kearnes, M., & Rickards, L. (2020). Knowing earth, knowing soil: Epistemological work and the political aesthetics of regenerative agriculture. In J. F. Salazar, C. Granjou, M. Kearnes, A. Krzywoszynska, & M. Tironi (Eds.), *Thinking with soils: Social theory and material politics* (pp. 71–88). Bloomsbury.

Klein, A., Bohannan, B., Jaffe, D., Levin, D., & Green, J. (2016). Molecular evidence for metabolically active bacteria in the atmosphere. *Frontiers in Microbiology, 7*. https://doi.org/10.3389/fmicb.2016.00772

Danjoo Koorliny. (2021). Noongar Land Enterprise Group opens new native tree nursery. *Danjoo Koorliny Walking Together*, June 2. Retrieved August 15, 2021, from https://www.danjookoorliny.com/post/noongar-land-enterprise-group-opens-new-native-plant-nursery

Krzywoszynska, A. (2020). Nonhuman labor and the making of resources: Making soils a resource through microbial labor. *Environmental Humanities, 12*(1), 227–249.

Lorimer, J. (2020). *The probiotic planet: Using life to manage life*. University of Minnesota Press.

Massy, C. (2017). *Call of the Reed Warbler: A new agriculture, a new earth*. University of Queensland Press.

Mayes, C. (2018). *Unsettling food politics: Agriculture, dispossession and sovereignty.* Rowman & Littlefield.
Meldrum, R. (2009). Subjectivity and plant domestication: Decoding the agency of vegetable food crops. *Subjectivity, 28*, 326–333.
Mikulak, M. (2013). *The politics of the pantry: Stories, food, and social change.* McGill-Queen's University Press.
Nestlé. (2021). Supporting regenerative agriculture. Nestlé. Retrieved August 14, 2021, from https://www.nestle.com/csv/global-initiatives/zero-environmental-impact/climate-change-net-zero-roadmap/regenerative-agriculture
Newton, P., Civita, N., Frankel-Goldwater, L., Bartel, K., & Johns, C. (2020). What is regenerative agriculture? A review of scholar and practitioner definitions based on processes and outcomes. *Frontiers in Sustainable Food Systems, 4.* https://doi.org/10.3389/fsufs.2020.577723
Patel, R., & Moore, J. (2018). *A history of the world in seven cheap things: A guide to capitalism, nature, and the future of the planet.* University of California Press.
Tsing, A. (2009). Supply chains and the human condition. *Rethinking Marxism, 21*(2), 148–176.
Tsing, A. (2015). *The mushroom at the end of the world: On the possibility of life in capitalist ruins.* Princeton University Press.
Tuck, E., & Yang, K. W. (2012). Decolonization is not a metaphor. *Decolonization: Indigeneity, Education & Society, 1*(1), 1–40.

CHAPTER 6

Reviving Community Agrarianism in Post-socialist China

Daren Shi-Chi Leung

Abstract Tasked with feeding 1.4 billion people, China often promotes its success in food security in relation to its self-sufficient grain production. In the post-socialist context, the reformist state has been pursuing a capital-based vertical model to integrate millions of smallholding producers into the market. Yet, the introduction of high-yield hybrid rice to increase production has resulted in a set of related crises, including widespread environmental pollution, food-safety issues and adverse impacts on rural life. However, agrarian communities are challenging these state-imposed practices of food production. This chapter explores an endogenous form of regenerative agriculture that has emerged in South China since the early 2000s, a Chinese form of food and farming activism for reviving community agrarianism. I argue that the revitalization of "traditional" farming practices as a form of *xaingtu* (rural) knowledge has evolved with and through local peasants' experience and struggle over the decades. One example that combines diverse aspects of such knowledge is the "fish-duck-rice paddy", a well-known symbiotic method of pest

D. S.-C. Leung (✉)
Department of Cultural Studies, Lingnan University, Tuen Mun, Hong Kong
e-mail: darenleung@LN.edu.hk

V. Stead, M. Hinkson (eds.), *Beyond Global Food Supply Chains*,
https://doi.org/10.1007/978-981-19-3155-0_6

control that also works with native varieties, organic manure and cooperative labour. This method revives peasants' experience of the Mao era as a cultural reference for *community* agrarianism. The revival of community agrarianism allows farming to be narrated as an evolving social and historical practice, not "wasting" peasants' knowledge, in contrast to the capitalist agrarian transformation.

Keywords Post-socialist China • Community-supported agriculture (CSA) • Rural knowledge • Farming methods • Peasantry • Agricultural commons

Introduction: Feeding China in Post-socialist Times

Today, China must feed nearly one-fifth of the world's population—1.4 billion people—with less than a tenth of its total farmland. Feeding China not only is a historical challenge in attempting to eliminate famine and hunger (Li, 1982) but also centres on a pressing series of contemporary issues, including declining farming labour, widespread environmental pollution and recurring risks of food safety. Chinese authorities, while aware of these issues, insist that "in the new era, the Chinese people are more concerned with their nutrition and health, from having enough food to eating well and safely" (State Council, 2019). Whether the Chinese can feed themselves or not, feeding China, with increasingly more and better-quality food, indeed poses a global challenge (The Economist Explains, 2015). To better understand this Chinese problem, it is necessary to take a perspective from the post-socialist period.

As China rejoined the world economy in the 1990s, some asked, "Who will feed China?" without threatening global food security and ecological sustainability (Brown, 1995). By saying, "Chinese people will feed themselves", the Chinese authorities promised the world that they would strengthen "the motivational force" via a market economy and expedite "scientific and technological advances" for increasing agricultural production of grain (State Council, 1996). The introduction of hybrid rice (*zajiao shuidao*) in the 1980s is an important case. The rice could be high-yielding and endure large quantities of inputs like synthetic fertilizers, pesticides and weed control. That "success" has served as a political and scientific promise in China's ongoing politics of food security, exemplified by the national celebration to mark the recent death of renowned rice geneticist Yuan Longping, also known as the "father of hybrid rice" (Schmalzer, 2021).

The promise of hybrid rice worked in conjunction with land reforms introduced from the 1980s. The new reformist state farewelled the socialist period (1950s–1970s) by introducing a "new socialist countryside". It dismantled collective agriculture, replacing communal production teams with the Household Responsibility Contract Scheme that instituted two-tiered land rights: land belonged to the village collective, while the right to use land was equally divided and land could be leased to families through a contract procurement system. While guaranteeing the state's plan for grain purchase, the state also insisted on new arrangements for organising millions of agricultural producers (He, 2017). The reformist model incorporated smallholders into a market that promoted modern farming technology and competition while maintaining a high level of food security. Over the years, combining modern farming technology (like hybrid rice) with the marketized organization of farmers has become the mainstream strategy for feeding China. Yet such reform has resulted in a set of rural crises, commonly known as the "three rural problems" (*sannongwenti*) interrelating peasant, village and agriculture (Wen, 2001).

The dilemma of how to feed China has revealed the recurrent conditions of farming in China: the land is collectively owned and farming methods are privatized. In the post-socialist context, socialism is no longer regarded as antagonistic to capitalism (Dirlik, 1989; Day, 2013, p. 15). Similarly, Huang et al. (2012, p. 140) have observed that Chinese agriculture moves towards neither capitalism nor socialism but towards "something different, along the lines of marketized cooperatives, in the manner originally envisioned [in the Chayanovian notion of peasant family farming]". He Xuefeng (2017) sees these new arrangements as questioning the peasants' way of life as historically grounded in the idea of a "household-based economy", which contracts the so-called small peasant economy in East Asian societies (like Japan, South Korea and Taiwan), whereas today farmland is more likely a profit-driven property resulting from the land-distribution policies of the Cold War period (He, 2017, pp. 5–6). In post-socialist China, farmland that is still collectively owned supports the most basic means of production that "allows householders focusing on agricultural production [instead of becoming rural-urban migrants]" and that "makes various forms of cooperation possible" (He, 2017, p. 7).

In this chapter, I explore the politics of food and farming in post-socialist China with an interest in *the possibilities for (re)organising farmers* in ways that vary from the state's capital-based vertical integration. My focus is on an alternative model that advocates for rural social revival. I undertake this exploration through a comparison of the cases of hybrid rice and eco-rice. I will examine an endogenous form of regenerative agriculture that has emerged in South China to argue that the revival of community agrarianism involves the creative preservation of practices peasants have carried forward from the socialist era, while resisting the reformist transformation of agriculture. Through this movement, a distinctive Chinese community-supported agriculture (CSA) has been taking shape and expanding.

The Reformist Model for Chinese Agricultural Problems

In order to solve poverty in the post-socialist period, the Chinese state introduced a reformist transformation of agriculture. It adopted a reformist discourse of "market socialism" that frames farming labour through access to capital-based methods of input and output (Huang et al., 2012, p. 142). The reform allowed the state to organize peasants differently, shifting from Mao-era rural integration of "commune-production teams-households" to the market-mediated linkage of "company-cooperatives-households" (Yan et al., 2020). In the 2000s, a series of vigorous agricultural and rural policies was launched to "streamline" and "scale up" the ineffective agricultural system (Day & Schneider, 2017). These policies include, first, the promotion of "dragon head enterprises"—the giant agribusinesses that can vertically integrate households with processing and product markets and agricultural technology; second, the implementation of the Law on Specialised Farmer Cooperative that groups householders as an economic unit producing the same product or using the same agricultural service (e.g. "one-village/cooperative-one-product"); and, last, the abolition of the agricultural tax to reduce the financial burden on peasants. This capital-led vertical integration of agriculture was recently reasserted by the 19th National Congress of the Chinese Communist Party in 2019 to continue the better linking of company, cooperative and households, while also celebrating its success in grain security, to bring "millions of small farmers onto the track of modern agricultural development" (State Council, 2019).

The reformist model tends to formulate "the problems of agricultural production as the most pressing issue for China" and "the capitalist, industrial forms of modernization as the most important solution", which paves the way to the rise of "agrarian capitalism" (Day & Schneider, 2017: p. 9; Yan et al., 2020). This capitalist transformation progresses the state's agenda of food security with a technocratic discourse that focuses on the alleviation of rural poverty and the increase of agricultural productivity. Over the years, vertical integration has introduced further industrial and modern farming technologies (e.g. high-yield seed, artificial inputs and machineries), tending towards homogenization of various agronomic practices across the country (Huang et al., 2012). As a result, the "three rural problems" have intensified. Specifically, the commodification of "the natural land and human resource on which people's livelihood depended" is expanding, as is capital-intensive, resource-intensive and chemical-intensive agriculture that "not only destroys nature and family but also homogenizes diversified rural indigenous traditional knowledge" (Wen et al., 2012, p. 31). This reformist model is, as Schneider (2017) concludes, "wasting the rural", because agricultural industrialization disregards the long-standing, ecologically concerned farming techniques, such as the use of organic manure, that Chinese farmers have worked with for centuries.

It is for these reasons that Chinese rural advocates have drawn public attention away from rural poverty to the trend of deteriorating culture and ecology in the countryside. One commonly posed question is how to "organise [rural people] to counter the power and emergence of capitalist hegemony within society and the market" (Day, 2013, p. 9). As He Xuefeng has argued (2017), the rural crisis is far more than an economic problem but rather a form of social disintegration of rural community. It comprises the following factors:

> the commodification of agricultural input, labour, public goods and technical service, a steady exodus of educated rural youth as migrants to cities, the aging and feminisation of rural producers, fragmentation of familial life, estrangement of social relations with villages, growing rural disparity, etc. (Yan & Chen, 2013, p. 964)

Thus, rural advocates have called for alternative approaches to rural development, considering the sustainability of agricultural production in relation to rural livelihood (and its reproduction) and the coherence of rural society (Yan & Chen, 2013). One attends to the emergence of alternative food chains with booming CSA initiatives, ranging from CSA farms, farmers markets and buying clubs, to farmer cooperatives. A form of rural activism is emerging through these activities, leading to "a more economically viable, ecologically embedded rural development model" (Si & Scott, 2016, p. 1094). Despite their limited scale, it is evident that CSA initiatives are improving the local environment through agricultural remediation (e.g. removing pollution and contaminants) and enhancing the social and economic value of farmland to prevent the expansion of non-farming purposes of urbanization and industrialization (Kurl & Ho, 2017, p. 844). Scott et al. (2018) summarize the movement as a kind of bottom-up food activism that brings together food safety and rural revival against the state-led technocratic discourse of ecological agriculture.

The Rise of the Agrarian Renaissance in South China

In my fieldwork on CSA in Guangzhou city, I found that it was common for grains like rice, wheat and millet to be sold at the monthly Guangzhou Farmers Market (*Chengxianghui*), in addition to fresh vegetables. "Eco-rice" is one such grain. It sells for double the price of regular rice, but consumers are keen to buy it in support of farmers growing native varieties in the countryside. Tracing the origins of eco-rice, I discovered what I term the "agrarian renaissance" movement in South China, an endogenous regenerative agricultural movement that "focuses on the revival of peasants' indigenous knowledge and respects peasant's livelihoods and the environment" (Leung, 2021, p. 31). Here, I dig into this more deeply to show that this revival involves reintroducing so-called traditional farming techniques and, in association with those techniques, peasants' Mao-era experience in the post-socialist context. I identify an evolving form of *xaingtu* knowledge that, according to Chinese ecological anthropologist He Jun's (2007) research on "indigenous environmental knowledge", rejects any static or binary thinking about traditional versus modern technologies. Rather, *xaingtu* involves a socio-material approach to understanding farming techniques resulting from peasants' local intergenerational experiences and struggles. Attention to *xaingtu* prompts questions about farming practices that have evolved across the shifting social organization of rural society.

The data for examining community agrarianism is drawn from archival materials, field observation and interviews I conducted through the network of Partnership of Community Development (PCD). Established in 2001 in Hong Kong, PCD has played a key role in the introduction of CSA to midland China. It has also documented ways "to explore, practice and evaluate" the grassroots farming projects against reformist and capitalist models of agriculture (PCD, 2019, p. 10). These projects were first trialled in South China, a traditional rice-growing region that was targeted by the state's project of technological transformation through the introduction of hybrid rice. According to his decade-long observation, Angus Lam (interview, 2019), who worked at Greenpeace from 1997 to 2007 and is now a project coordinator of PCD, points out that the mainstream strategy for improving rural livelihoods "brings in modern technologies such as chemical fertilisers, hybrid seeds, and even invasive eucalyptus timber available from the market" that "resulted in wrecking local farmland, like some terraced field collapses due to soil erosion". Meanwhile, Lam continues, some rural actors and groups from the fields of environmental protection, indigenous agricultural research, social work and so on, "began to attend to traditional farming knowledge with the approach of regenerative or multifunctional agriculture". In the early 2000s, PCD launched a series of participatory-action research projects by recruiting villagers, local cadres and researchers as the "community facilitators" to explore and document peasants' oral histories, their struggles with recent rural decline, and traditional farming techniques they continued to practise (PCD, 2005, 2019).

These pilot projects found that the historical root of "traditional" farming had been integrated into the collectivist agriculture of the socialist era, also known as Mao's era, challenging its popular impression of "cultural deconstruction" or "cultural homogenisation" (PCD, 2007, pp. 72, 94). The cultural exploration revealed a dynamic relationship between peasants' livelihoods, food production techniques and the health of the environment, preserving what Schmalzser (2016) calls the indigenous knowledge of Maoist China. It emphasized the public service provisioned by the collective labour that was once maintained by the "work-point" system under village-based production teams and that was threatened by the disorganization of peasants in the reform era (He, 2017). Collective labour had long supported the establishment and maintenance of irrigation (wheel watering, reservoirs, canals) in the rice paddies (PCD, 2007, p. 67). It also supported customary techniques of using manure to improve soil health. The transformation in manure work provides a narrative of shifting rural knowledge. It allows us to trace the changes in the social practices of farming through peasants' perspectives and experiences in relation to their livelihood dynamics, via the shifting use of chemical and organic manure.

According to Shi Sheungde (PCD, 2007), one of PCD's community facilitators, there were diverse native methods for the production of organic manure drawn from peasants' experience of Mao's era long before the introduction of chemical fertilizers in 1985. For example, manure (*fei*) was a combination of fermented manure mixed with human waste, livestock waste and weeds that was composted for a week to fully ferment as ripe manure (p. 56). In addition, peasants were able to experiment with different kinds of green manure (*lvfei)* on collective farms. They became proficient in techniques of cultivation and crop rotation to improve different soil conditions, in both dry and wet fields (p. 55). "This knowledge", as Shi points out, "is not only passed down from fathers to sons but is also common knowledge that people have been practising for a long time" (p. 56). Peasants are turning back to these techniques to deal with problems like caked soil, frequent pests, disease and even slowing yields, all caused by their adoption of modern farming. As Shi observes:

> Most peasants are now using a mixed form of planting, and all dry fields are planted with green manure, except for the time of severe drought. This is a widely used technique for supplementing rice soil fertility for the local peasants combined with local skills and alien crops [e.g. hybrid rice]. Since the 1990s, the technique of [green manure] has matured and, in the lack of farmyard manure, it has become an important component of the local agricultural system, a key strategy that does not overly rely on chemical fertilisers. (PCD, 2007, p. 56)

This agrarian narrative highlights the knowledge of farming inherited from the socialist era and deployed by peasants to negotiate with modern farming techniques in the post-socialist time (He, 2007). However, some also suggest that those customary farming practices are regarded as useless and even forgotten by peasants under the hegemony of modern farming (also see PCD, 2008, p. 13; Dominelli & Ku, 2017).

There are numerous examples collected by PCD and related organizations that demonstrate that peasants are the active subjects initiating and innovating with such knowledge to navigate rural problems as they arise. The body of knowledge ranges across attitudes of stewardship, preferences for farming local varieties, pest prevention, the sharing of experience, cooperative labour and so on. One of the best examples of a suite of

Fig. 6.1 A native breed of ducks working on a fish-duck-rice paddy in Qiandongnan Miao and Dong Autonomous Prefecture, Guizhou. (Images provided by Xiangdang)

techniques that demonstrates the holistic application of such knowledge is the "fish-duck-rice paddy", or *yuyadao* (see Fig. 6.1). This is a well-known symbiotic method of pest control that replaces weedicide and pesticide with a traditional method that employs fish and ducks in the field to consume pests and weeds. It works effectively in rotation with green manure (PCD, 2007, pp. 55, 67; also see Dai & Xue, 2019). For PCD (2019, p. 77), if such knowledge is revitalized, the community-based component would help local people and CSA practitioners to explore the historical changes in their village life while broadening the basis of sustainable community development.

The agrarian renaissance movement in South China renders the revival of peasants' Mao-era experience visible via the continuing practice of traditional, native or indigenous farming techniques. Rather than disappearing, these customary agricultural practices are thriving. As I argue, the approach of *xaingtu* knowledge is socially engaged and historically grounded in particular ways. It emphasizes the agency of peasants' collective innovation in "native methods" (peasants here refer to *tufangfa*, a Maoist term, expressed with nostalgia) to transform their local conditions (also see Schmalzer, 2018, p. 9). The embrace of *xaingtu* suggests an alternative approach to organizing peasants—as a form of community making that privileges livelihood and the environment rather than the "wasting" of "the rural" that occurs in reformist developments. For rural advocates, the practice of *xaingtu* knowledge ultimately reveals social foundations for promoting community agrarianism in which villagers and CSA practitioners enact a new collective form of household farming in the post-socialist countryside. Working in support of a different form of economy, commonly known as "community economy" in the field of sustainable rural development, is a key challenge for revitalizing indigenous farming knowledge like "fish-duck-rice paddy" (Dominelli & Ku, 2017; Wen et al., 2012). As a result, reviving community agrarianism often involves grouping farmers together in mutual-aid groups and cooperatives (PCD, 2019). This contrasts with the state-led specialized farmers' cooperative, which, as another project coordinator of PCD, Edwin Chan (interview, 2018), states, is an economic unit lacking "a culture of cooperation" for community development.

The Rural–Urban Challenge for Sustaining Community Agrarianism

What distinguishes the Chinese CSA movement's practice of community agrarianism is its alternative approach to the production of grain (specifically, rice) and the shifting experience of village peasants in relation to the changing history of socialism. This agricultural activity needs to be understood as distinct from the increasing number of family-based CSA farms with consumer members operated by passionate so-called new farmers who return from cities (Si & Scott, 2016). There is also a big challenge to improve rural–urban relationships by reconnecting producers and consumers in support of sustaining community economies. One of the urban obstacles goes to the prevailing context of food-safety problems. Recurring food scandals produce public anxiety and lack of trust in China's chaotic conventional food chains, while leaving space for so-called emerging alternative food chains to flourish (Leung, 2021; Scott et al., 2014; Veeck et al., 2010). Yet, civil authorities attempt to regain public trust in their promotion of safe, quality food sourced from urban communities, in contrast to the progressive but still ineffective state-led food-safety policy (Leung, 2021; Scott et al., 2018).

Due to such high levels of public distrust, Kelvin Wang (interview, 2019), a rural social worker organising eco-rice cooperatives in Yunnan, still remembers that when CSA commenced, it often experienced poor sales. The movement lacked the capacity to engage consumers (also see PCD, 2013, p. 97). This set of challenges led to PCD establishing a flagship programme of CSA internships in rural initiatives in the mid-2000s in an attempt to improve rural–urban relationships and incubate a number of young food activists to better engage with the ever-shifting urban culture. As CSA interns report, successful examples of promoting practices like rice, duck and fish occurred when they connected with consumers' (e.g. housewives') everyday shopping experience for food safety and quality (see PCD, 2008, pp. 10–12; 2009, p. 17; 2014, p. 158). Since then, CSA activists have attempted to build a stronger network at the rural–urban nexus (PCD, 2008). Over time, they have responded effectively to challenges of urban consumption, including food scares.

In recent years, there has been an emergence of urban-based consumer-led groups focused on incorporating urban people into the ways of caring for rural communities via food production. Wang Xiangdang (interview, 2018), a CSA intern, formed Farmers' Friend in 2006 in Liuzhou, Guangxi, and points out the significance of the involvement of urban consumers in its rapid development: "while demanding safe and quality food, consumers can also be passionate, resourceful, and creative in initiating a consumer-producer connection via organising farmer's market and buying club". Another more convivial case is in Guangdong. According to Rao Qihong (interview, 2018), another CSA intern, Guangzhou Farmers Market was founded in 2009 originally to promote eco-rice, where "we use it to make sushi which consumers could try and trust themselves". Over time, consumers who become volunteers and even organizers have developed a more participatory method to promote a consumer–producer connection in what I call "convivial agriculture" (Leung, 2021, p. 32). Recently, the group has been more ambitious in organising the Canton Harvest Festival (*fengnianqing*) that brings together rural initiatives from across five provinces in South China (see Fig. 6.2).

By examining the case of PCD, which has nurtured food and farming activists from community facilitators to CSA interns, we have seen how community agrarianism develops in and through localized CSA practice. CSA now reaches through the networks of the agrarian renaissance

Fig. 6.2 Poster for the Canton Harvest Festival in 2019 showing the theme of eco-rice

movement in the countryside, in the exchange of knowledge, resources and experiences to promote ecological farming, and then extends to urban areas, where consumers are encouraged to search for ways to participate in processes of production. Community agrarianism is thus taking up the challenge to transform rural–urban relations. Beyond a set of farming techniques, it is a method for making a shared, sustainable agricultural environment.

Conclusion: What We Have Shared Through Growing Food?

Community agrarianism is a distinctive arm of the Chinese CSA movement in post-socialist China. Adopting the approach of *xiangtu* has enabled farmers to apply "traditional" knowledge to positively transform the conditions under which they farm. Furthermore, this approach opens out to a wider collective effort to, as my interviewee Lam insists, "create the 'commons' for all of us". Romanticized as it might be, creating a commons, in line with J.K. Gibson-Graham's post-capitalist perspective, is also a process of forming "community". It is a process of negotiating "the quintessentially ethical concerns … of how we are living together" (Gibson-Graham, 2006a, p. 82) and that involves "struggle, uncertainty, ambivalence, and disappointment" and discards "any fantasy that there is a perfect community economy" (Gibson-Graham, 2006b, p. xv). Throughout my fieldwork, I have observed long-standing food activists enter these food scenes between the countryside and cities with joy and encouragement, though sometimes with frustration and difficulty. In support of the "commons", peasants like Xiaoyue (interview, 2019), who struggle to fully adopt organic farming, put it simply but profoundly, "I feel proud of our hard work of farming that can feed the healthy land and feed healthy people".

Commoning the environment can be approached by rural and urban communities through shared interests in food. As I and others have argued, an "agricultural commons" (Cameron, 2015; Leung, 2021) should take into account the preservation of agrarian knowledge as a basis for improving consumer–producer relationships. Such an approach offers localized knowledge in support of the booming trend of CSA farms and related cooperatives across the country (Cook, 2016). In addition, it can fuel a wave of community economies for rural revival through hacking ideas of ecological agriculture promoted by the state (Scott et al., 2014) that have often failed or that failed to account for the diverse farming practices of small-scale producers and the environmental concerns of consumers.

References

Brown, L. R. (1995). *Who will feed China?: Wake-up call for a small planet.* Earthscan.

Cameron, J. (2015). Enterprise innovation and economic diversity in community-supported agriculture: Sustaining the agricultural commons. In G. Roelvink, K. S. Martin, & J. K. Gibson-Graham (Eds.), *Making other worlds possible: Performing diverse economies.* University of Minnesota Press.

Cook, S.. (2016). *Nurturing the shoots of China's sustainable agriculture.* International Institute for Environment and Development, March 23.

Dai, R., & Xue, D. (2019). *Of rice, fish, ducks and humans.* UNESCO Courier, January. https://en.unesco.org/courier/2019-1/rice-fish-ducks-and-humans

Day, A. F. (2013). *The peasant in Postsocialist China.* Cambridge University Press.

Day, A. F., & Schneider, M. (2017). The end of alternatives? Capitalist transformation, rural activism and the politics of possibility in China. *Journal of Peasant Studies, 45*(7), 1221–1246.

Dirlik, A. (1989). Postsocialism? Reflection on 'socialism with Chinese Characteristics'. In A. Dirlik & M. J. Meisner (Eds.), *Marxism and the Chinese experience: Issues in contemporary Chinese Socialism.* M.E. Sharpe.

Dominelli, L., & Ku, H.-b. (2017). Green social work and its implications for social development in China. *China Journal of Social Work, 10*(1), 3–22.

Gibson-Graham, J. K. (2006a). *The end of Capitalism (as we knew it): A feminist critique of political economy.* University of Minnesota Press.

Gibson-Graham, J. K. (2006b). *Postcapitalist politics.* University of Minnesota Press.

He, J. (2007). Indigenous knowledge and cultural reflection. In *Thinking of soil: Traditional culture and rural construction*, ed. PCD. PCD. (In Chinese)

He, X. (2017). On the advantages of rural land collective ownership. *Journal of Nanjing Agricultural University (Social Sciences Edition), 17*(3), 1–8. (In Chinese).

Huang, P. C. C., Gao, Y., & Peng, Y. (2012). Capitalization without proletarianization in China's agricultural development. *Modern China, 38*(2), 139–173.

Kurl, K., & Ho, P. (2017). Alternative approaches to food: Community supported agriculture in urban China. *Sustainability (Switzerland), 9*(5), 1–16.

Leung, D. S.-C. (2021). Convivial agriculture: Evolving food and farming activism in South China. *China Perspectives, 2*, 29–38.

Li, L. M. (1982). Introduction: Food, famine, and the Chinese state. *The Journal of Asian Studies, 41*(4), 687–707.

PCD. (2005). *Partnerships for Community Development 2002–2005*. PCD. (In Chinese).
PCD. (2007). *Thinking of soil: Traditional culture and rural construction*. PCD. (In Chinese).
PCD. (2008). *Fragrant soil*. Issue 1. (In Chinese)
PCD. (2009). *Fragrant soil*. Issue 2. (In Chinese)
PCD. (2013). *Taking roots: The revival of community-supported agriculture*. PCD. (In Chinese).
PCD. (2014). *Fragrant soil*. Issue 6. (In Chinese)
PCD. (2019). *Cultural reflection on agriculture: The notebook of facilitators*. PCD. (In Chinese).
Schmalzer, S. (2016). *Red Revolution, Green Revolution: Scientific farming in Socialist China*. University of Chicago Press.
Schmalzer, S. (2018). Toward a transnational, trans-1978 history of food politics in China: An exploratory paper. *The PRC History Review, 3*(1), 1–14.
Schmalzer, S. (2021). Beholding Yuan Longping in the light of recent Chinese history. *Positions Politics*, June 24. Retrieved August 21, 2021, from https://positionspolitics.org/sigrid-schmalzer-beholding-yuan-longping-in-the-light-of-recent-chinese-history
Schneider, M. (2017). Wasting the rural: Meat, manure, and the politics of agro-industrialization in contemporary China. *Geoforum, 78*, 89–97.
Scott, S., Si, Z., Schumilas, T., & Chen, A. (2014). Contradictions in state- and civil society-driven developments in China's ecological agriculture sector. *Food Policy, 45*, 158–166.
Scott, S., Si, Z., Schumilas, T., & Chen, A. (2018). *Organic food and farming in China: Top-down and bottom-up ecological initiatives*. Routledge.
Si, Z., & Scott, S. (2016). The convergence of alternative food networks within 'rural development' initiatives: The case of the new rural reconstruction movement in China. *Local Environment, 21*(9), 1082–1099.
State Council Information Office of the People's Republic of China. (1996). *The grain issue in China*. White Papers of the Government.
State Council Information Office of the People's Republic of China. (2019). *Food security in China*. White Papers of the Government.
The Economist Explains. (2015). China's inefficient agricultural system. *The Economist*, May 21.
Veeck, A., Hongyan, Y., & Burns, A. C. (2010). Consumer risks and new food systems in urban China. *Journal of Macromarketing, 30*(3), 222–237.
Wen, T. (2001). Centenary reflections on the 'three dimensional problem' of rural China. *Inter-Asia Cultural Studies, 2*(2), 287–295.
Wen, T., Lau, K., Cheng, C., & He, H. (2012). Ecological civilization, indigenous culture, and rural reconstruction in China. *Monthly Review, 63*(9), 29–35.

Yan, H., & Chen, Y. (2013). Debating the rural cooperative movement in China, the past and the present. *Journal of Peasant Studies, 40*(6), 955–981.
Yan, H., Hok-bun, K., & Siyuan, X. (2020). Rural revitalization, scholars, and the dynamics of the collective future in China. *Journal of Peasant Studies, 48*(4), 853–874.

PART III

Distribution

CHAPTER 7

Fantasies of Logistics in Aotearoa New Zealand

Matthew Henry and Carolyn Morris

Abstract Logistics is a form of calculative reasoning and set of material practices framed by the fantasy of perpetual, seamless circulation. This fantasy is built on ideas of universal connection and fungibility that sit beyond the teeming messiness of lived, unpacified life. The fantasy of connection is, however, continually haunted by an anxiety that an irruption of liveliness will disrupt material flows and expectations of plenitude. In this chapter, we draw on two case studies of food disruption from Aotearoa New Zealand—pork and flour—to interrogate these promises. The two cases take the form of vignettes when the regular operation of logistics relationships was in some way affected by the COVID-19 response of the Aotearoa New Zealand government and other actors. We argue that the character and impact of the disruption experienced in each case study are specific to its material and cultural particularities and that the particularities of disruption themselves provide a valuable analytical entry point for understanding the fragility and contingency of logistics. This leads us to show that the critical analysis of logistics relationships needs to move beyond a

M. Henry (✉) • C. Morris
School of People, Environment and Planning, Massey University, Palmerston North, New Zealand
e-mail: M.G.Henry@massey.ac.nz; C.M.Morris@massey.ac.nz

V. Stead, M. Hinkson (eds.), *Beyond Global Food Supply Chains*,
https://doi.org/10.1007/978-981-19-3155-0_7

mirroring of claims to universality and is more insightful when it is attentive to the specific materialities of things and their liveliness.

Keywords Aotearoa New Zealand • Pork • Animal welfare • Flour • Packaging • Materialities

Introduction

Logistics is a form of calculative reasoning and associated material practices framed by fantasies of perpetual, seamless circulation resulting in unfailing and unending plenitude whenever and wherever it is desired. These fantasies are built on ideas of universal connection and fungibility where the goal is to tame and control the teeming messiness of lived, unpacified life. Such logistics imaginaries animate the extraordinarily complex supply chains that coordinate producers, processors, manufacturers, transporters and retailers to deliver (for the middle classes at least) a perpetual and seamless supply of food. When supply chains work as they are supposed to, "the entire network of infrastructures, technologies, spaces, workers, and violence that makes the circulation of stuff possible remains tucked out of sight for those who engage with logistics only as consumers" (Cowen, 2014, p. 1). And what is generated for such lucky consumers is a lifeworld that can be taken for granted, producing subjective, social and cultural security—what Law (2014) terms the miracle of things working.

However, logistics and supply chains rarely work as seamlessly as hoped and claimed (Neilson, 2012). While logistics operations aim to fashion homogenous, fungible networks, they are continually haunted by the threats of frictions and disruptions that plague logistics in practice (Gregson, 2017, Gregson, Crang and Antonopoulos, 2017). The result is as Chua et al. (2018, p. 623) warn: "we should be careful not to reify logistics as a seamless system of instantaneous flow and total functional integration". Instead, they argue, scholars need to pay attention to the liveliness of logistics, the ceaseless work done to pacify that liveliness, and the vulnerabilities created from the calculative, material and spatial practices of circulation.

The labour of pacifying commodities into networks called "logistics" and "supply chains" that can be imagined and experienced as stable, predictable, controllable and enduring is Sisyphean, and the results can be undone by things both big and small, human and non-human. This is because non-human actants have what Jane Bennett (2010, p. viii) calls "vitality"—that is, they have the capacity "not only to impede or block the will and designs of humans but also to act as quasi agents or forces with trajectories, propensities, or tendencies of their own". This vitality, or agency, stems from what she calls their *thing-power* (Bennett, 2010, p. vxi). Vitalities, vulnerabilities, threats and disruptions are actually always materially and culturally particular, and it is by paying close attention to particularities that the contingency, instability and labour of assembling particular supply chains becomes apparent.

In this chapter, we explore the causes and consequences of two COVID-19-generated supply-chain disruptions in Aotearoa New Zealand: those affecting pork and flour. What these events demonstrate is that disruptions are not singular, unidirectional or purely economic, as the discourse about supply chains and logistics might suggest. The pork disruption caused an economic problem for the industry, but a different problem for butchers and pig farmers (and processors and importers). The problem for butchers was managing inventory, but the problem for farmers was the constant birth of piglets. Their sows' fecundity was also an animal welfare problem, which is why the government intervened to repair the supply chain. The flour disruption, by contrast, was a consumer disruption and a disruption to subjectivities. The problem was how to get enough flour to make home-made sourdough to photograph for Facebook and Instagram—it was a problem of performing a certain kind of class and family identity.

COVID-19 in Aotearoa New Zealand

When examining systems that seem to run seamlessly, it is imperative not to be seduced by the system's logics, as though those logics effortlessly translate into actually existing relationships. We need to pay attention to turbulence, liveliness and particularity in logistics, and these ideas apply equally to the wider contexts within which these supply chains emerge and perform. Aotearoa New Zealand has had (and continues to have) a very particular experience of COVID-19 and its impacts. The strategy was to "go hard and go early" and eliminate the virus. Despite the tragedy of individual deaths (26 in the first wave), there has not been the horror of mass death, and Aotearoa New Zealanders have come to live with and, on the whole, willingly accept strict controls on their movements and give support to the government's shift from a business focus to one primarily concerned with public health. Indeed, we finalized this chapter under the conditions of a second national lockdown that was swiftly announced and almost universally seen as prophylactic necessity.

On 28 February 2020 the first case of COVID-19 entered Aotearoa New Zealand via a woman returning from Iran, and cases continued to grow quickly through March. The country's borders were closed to non-citizens and non-residents on 19 March, and on 21 March the government announced a plan to deal with COVID-19 via a four-level alert system, with increasingly strict restrictions imposed at each level. On 23 March the government announced that in 48 hours' time (at 11.59 pm on 25 March), Aotearoa New Zealand would move into level-four lockdown for a minimum of four weeks. This meant that all educational institutions and non-essential businesses and workplaces were closed, and people were instructed to isolate themselves in their own homes. Passed as an emergency response, the *COVID-19 Public Health Response Act* 2020 granted the government extraordinary powers to enforce lockdown regulations, the extent of which had not been seen outside of wartime. During the lockdown, essential businesses, including supermarkets but not all food retailers, remained open, while export-oriented agricultural processors continued to operate. It was the lockdown specifically that disrupted the pork and flour chains, requiring (and achieving) reordering.

Too Many Pigs

For a country that exports 85 per cent of the meat that it produces, pork production is anomalous because the 600,000 pigs raised each year (by fewer than 100 commercial growers) are solely destined for the domestic market (NZ Pork, 2020). From peaks through the 1930s and 1960s, domestic pork production has become an increasingly marginal activity, with significant declines in piggeries and pig numbers caused by static demand and the loss of cheap feed (whey) from the dairy industry. Indeed, Aotearoa New Zealand has become a pork importer, with almost 60 per cent of pork and 85 per cent of cured products such as bacon coming from cheaper large-scale producers in places such as Australia, Spain and the United States (NZ Pork, 2020).

Before COVID-19, the risks experienced by pig farmers already encompassed competition, animal welfare and biosecurity anxieties (NZ Pork, 2020). The African Swine Fever (ASF) pandemic that re-erupted in 2018 resulted in the pre-emptive slaughter of millions of pigs across China, creating fears in the pig industry that the disease might enter Aotearoa New Zealand via pork imports (Standaert, 2020). The cheapness of imported pork, driven by economies of scale, was placing domestic pork producers under financial pressure, and this pressure was amplified by public campaigns against rearing practices such as farrowing crates. One response to these pressures, led by the industry's statutory board, NZ Pork, was a campaign for the introduction of mandatory country-of-origin labelling to counter the persistent invisibility of pork imports for domestic consumers (NZ Pork, 2020). However, despite the campaign's success, the introduction of the new labelling laws was an early casualty of COVID-19's emergence in Aotearoa New Zealand as the government's energies shifted to counter the impact of the pandemic.

Aotearoa New Zealand's domestic pig farmers funnel their production through three main processors, Freshpork, Five Star Pork and Wilson Hellaby, which in turn supply supermarkets, retail butchers and the hospitality sector. The level-four lockdown of March 2021 required all non-essential businesses to close. In the days prior to the national lockdown, there had been heavy buying of a range of foodstuffs, including meat. This splurge had encouraged retail butchers to order additional supplies on the assumption that they would remain open over any lockdown as an essential service. However, the government drew a very tight boundary around what it deemed to be essential, and both butchers and the hospitality sector found themselves outside that boundary as supermarket-centric logistics, and supply networks were prioritized (*Fortune*, 2020).

At the stroke of a pen, the definition of retail butchers as non-essential created an immediate issue for butchers as to how to get rid of their excess stock and a looming challenge for pig processors and farmers (Martin, 2020). Just as retail butchers found that they could not get rid of pork, pigs continued to be ready for slaughter. As well as being distinctive by being domestically focused, the pork industry is different from other red meat supply chains in that it is not tightly organized around seasonal rhythms of supply: the pork industry has evolved to supply a continuous flow of meat all year round. This particular relationship to time is materially embedded in infrastructures such as freezers and piggeries. Prior to lockdown, 12,000 pigs were being killed weekly, and the closure of retail butchers, restaurants and so on meant a surplus of 5000 pigs per week (NZ Pork, 2020). Freezing pig carcasses and holding them in cold storage was an immediate response, but in a trade shaped by the logics of ceaseless flow and just-enough storage, freezer space quickly filled up. A system that delivered plenitude began to choke on its own surplus as pig numbers in piggeries burgeoned and consumer demand fell away with cafes and restaurants closed. This was enough to trigger widespread animal welfare concerns about the overcrowding of pigs and the threat of pigs being euthanized inhumanely at piggeries (which would in turn have generated the problem of the uncomfortable optics of carcass disposal).

Intense lobbying by the pig industry failed to achieve the redefinition of retail butchers as essential, and the problem of the surplus continued to grow through lockdown. However, other ways of managing the surplus emerged out of discussions between industry and government (Rae, 2020). The majority of Aotearoa New Zealand's pork is imported, and those imports were themselves being disrupted by the strains being placed on global shipping connections. Much of the imported pork was used by domestically based processing companies such as Wilson Hellaby to manufacture small goods such as bacon and ham (much to the pre-COVID-19 annoyance of pork farmers). The government and NZ Pork lobbied importers and processors to prioritize the use of local, fresh pork over frozen imported pork. This rerouting of pork flows was unusual in that it represented a renewed willingness of state agencies to become involved in questions of logistics that had been traditionally marked off as the preserve of private companies. The active role of the state in redefining and rerouting food-supply networks reached a peak in May 2020, when the government announced a scheme where it would buy 2000 surplus pigs a week, process them and distribute the meat to Maori *iwi*, community organizations and food banks. By August 2020, the government had spent $5.7 million and produced the equivalent of 1.7 million meals for distribution to over half a million people (Malthus, 2020). In a quiet but telling moment, the state had actively intervened to resolve a problem of oversupply. In this episode, the enduring instability of food systems, when confronted with the task of reconciling the needs of material bodies, limited infrastructure and the thwarted logics of flow, was illuminated.

The "Great" Flour Shortage of 2020

Media reports on 31 March 2020 said that stories of flour shortages were circulating on Facebook and Twitter (Kirkness, 2020). The reason for the shortage was initially identified as unnecessary panic-buying: "There's enough flour to go around, people are just buying it too fast, ANZ supermarkets say. It has forced the country's major supermarket chains to again plead with the public not to panic-buy, purchasing only what they need" (Kirkness, 2020, sentence 1–2). By the next day, a supply-chain cause of the shortage was identified. However, this was not a problem with the supply of milling wheat or a problem with milling capacity.

Retail flour—that is, flour sold directly to consumers—normally accounts for less than 10 per cent of the 225,000 tonnes of flour milled annually in Aotearoa New Zealand, with the majority being distributed by tanker to bread manufacturers and the rest delivered in 20-kilogramme bags to smaller bakeries (Lawrence, 2020). What flour millers were experiencing was a surge in demand for domestic-sized packages of flour. Farmers Mill in Timaru, for example, reported that within a few weeks, it had packaged the quantity of 5 kilogramme flour bags it would usually pack in four years (Lawrence, 2020). Similarly, Champion Flour reported a 500 per cent increase in demand for small-bagged flour (Checkpoint, 2020), and supermarket chain Foodstuffs reported that between mid-May and mid-June 2021, it had sold 1500 tonnes more flour than it had in the same period of the previous year (New Zealand Flour Millers Association, 2020). Despite the fact that 75 per cent of Aotearoa New Zealand's milling flour is imported from Australia, there was no reported disruption to the supply of flour itself. Instead, the disruption to the domestic flour supply chain was caused by lack of packaging rather than lack of flour: "Getting packaging normally took anywhere from six to nine weeks so the issue was not producing the flour, it was how to get the flour produced into small packages and into the supermarkets" (Lawrence, 2020, sentence 9).

The question then shifted from the causes of the shortage to the causes of the demand, and cultural explanations emerged. The dominant narrative was that Aotearoa New Zealanders were enacting a more "traditional" family life in the altered domestic conditions that lockdown produced:

> Many Kiwis have been posting their frustration and bewilderment about the lack of flour as they reignite the cooking days of old. Uber Eats and McDonald's have been taken away, so many parents are dragging their children to the stove top to see what they can create together. (Feek, 2020, sentence 3–4)

> The cafes aren't open, the restaurants aren't open, we've got children at home, we're locked down and we're looking to reconnect with our home baking, which is wonderful in the long-term. (Checkpoint, 2020, sentence 7)

Another commentator wrote that the lockdown provided "a great excuse to get into the kitchen as a family and do some from scratch cooking that we probably didn't have time to do pre-lockdown. Whatever the reason, convenience seemed to have taken a back seat during lockdown as Kiwis rediscovered their inner bakers, she said" (New Zealand Flour Millers Association, 2020, sentence 8–9).

Within a couple of days, the story had disappeared from the mainstream media, but it continued to circulate on social media, where people shared intelligence about which shops still had flour. A little smugly, those with flour posted photos of the cakes and bread they had baked. Partly because of the flurry of media attention, the flour shortage was in some ways an enjoyable experience. The government's decision to eradicate the virus had protected the population from the brutal realities of sickness and death that characterized many countries' experience of the pandemic, and most people were freed from pressing economic insecurity by income-support schemes, so for many Aotearoa New Zealanders the lockdown was quite exciting—we were part of the most important thing happening globally: we were having a COVID-19-caused shortage. Within 10 days or so, the shortage was over. I suspect that what happened was that people who wanted flour had stockpiled enough—18 months later, one of the authors of this chapter (Carolyn) has almost managed to use up the flour they bought at the beginning of the lockdown, while the other (Matt) has 10 kilogrammes still waiting to be used.

The flour shortage was brief, and there was no shortage of manufactured bread and baked goods at the supermarket (i.e. no one suddenly went hungry). From a consumer point of view, the flour supply chain somehow magically repaired itself.

The flour supply-chain disruption was not a problem with flour but with a taken-for-granted but overlooked actor in the chain: a particular size of paper bag. It was not so much a disruption for the industry, and in fact the shortage was in all likelihood a boon to flour producers, as consumers not only bought more flour than usual but bought greater quantities because of the lack of small bags. Instead, the disruption was a consumer one, caused by a run on flour as Aotearoa New Zealanders in lockdown sought comfort (and something to do) by baking. What was disrupted was not so much actual lived life but two fantasies: the fantasy of subjective and familial security promised by home baking as a way to deal with the profound insecurity generated by COVID-19 and the fantasy of unfailing plenitude promised by supply-chain capitalism.

Conclusion

These two small and comparatively insignificant cases of disruption provide a valuable analytical entry point for understanding how actually existing supply chains work—as opposed to the fantasies of how they are supposed to work. Just as supply chains are particular, so too are the things that disrupt them. The overarching disruption was COVID-19, but it was the lockdown that was imposed to eliminate the virus that was the proximate cause of the disruptions. In the case of pork, lockdown severed consumer access to a set of retail networks, and, in the case of flour, generated a surge in demand, animated by the desire to perform certain subjectivities. And the actors and their thing power that actually disrupted the supply chains were particular (and non-human): in the case of flour, it was the absence of correctly sized paper bags; in the case of pork, it was pig liveness and the fact that the sows continued to blithely birth, unaffected in their reproductive impulses, which did not shut down even as human social and economic life did. Both cases illustrate the problems generated by the practices of trying to meet the promises of perpetual plenitude: Fordist pork production, the everyday miracle of the replenishment of the supermarket shelves, and the bewilderment that ensued when the magic no longer worked. The ceaseless labour of pacifying commodities into supply chains is usually invisible, but it was revealed by these disruptions. However, the flour chain repaired itself and within a few days the shortage was over. The pork chain, by contrast, presented a more critical challenge (because pigs are living animals) and so the state intervened to stop an animal welfare disaster, an unusual step in an economy that prides itself on its neoliberal, market credentials, especially in relation to food and agriculture. What these small events show is that critical analysis of logistics relationships needs to move beyond a mirroring of claims to universality. Great insights are generated through attention to the specific materialities of things and their liveliness.

References

Bennett, J. (2010). *Vibrant matter: A political ecology of things*. Duke University Press.

Checkpoint. (2020, April 2). Covid-19: Flour demand up 500 percent for NZ producer, but plenty of wheat. *RNZ*. Retrieved August 18, 2021, from https://www.rnz.co.nz/national/programmes/checkpoint/audio/2018741266/covid-19-flour-demand-up-500-percent-for-nz-producer-but-plenty-of-wheat

Chua, C., Danyluk, M., Cowen, D., & Khalili, L. (2018). Introduction: Turbulent circulation: Building a critical engagement with logistics. *Environment and Planning D: Society and Space, 36*(4), 617–629. https://doi.org/10.1177/0263775818783101

Cowen, D. (2014). *The deadly life of logistics: Mapping violence in global trade*. University of Minnesota Press.

Feek, B. (2020, April 2). Covid 19 coronavirus: "We've got the flour", however, country-wide distribution proves tricky. *New Zealand Herald*. https://www.nzherald.co.nz/nz/covid-19-coronavirus-weve-got-the-flour-however-country-wide-distribution-proves-tricky/Z67QO42FVUCWLAOEIY4PYZ7K3U/

Fortune, A. (2020, March 25). New Zealand butcher shops deemed 'non-essential'. *FoodNavigator -Asia*.

Gregson, N. (2017). Logistics at work: Trucks, containers and the friction of circulation in the UK. *Mobilities, 12*(3), 343–364. https://doi.org/10.1080/17450101.2015.1087680

Gregson, N., Crang, M., & Antonopoulos, C. N. (2017). Holding together logistical worlds: Friction, seams and circulation in the emerging "global warehouse". *Environment and Planning D: Society and Space, 35*(3), 381–398. https://doi.org/10.1177/0263775816671721

Kirkness, L. (2020, March 31). Covid 19 coronavirus: What happened to all of New Zealand's flour? *New Zealand Herald*. https://www.nzherald.co.nz/nz/covid-19-coronavirus-what-happened-to-all-of-new-zealands-flour/FIRBD7KLO4V6AYJ6Q2ENO5VLGM/

Law, J. (2014). *Working well with wickedness*. CRESC Working Paper No. 135. Milton Keynes: Centre for Research on Socio-Cultural Change.

Lawrence, K. (2020, April 1). Coronavirus: Where has all the flour gone? *Stuff*. https://www.stuff.co.nz/life-style/well-good/120694953/coronavirus-where-has-all-the-flour-gone

Malthus, N. (2020, August 12). Hungry Kiwis pig out on free NZ pork during lockdown. *Rural News*.

Martin, R. (2020, March 31). Millions of dollars worth of meat headed to landfill due to trading ban. *RNZ*. https://www.rnz.co.nz/news/national/413077/millions-of-dollars-worth-of-meat-headed-to-landfill-due-to-trading-ban

Neilson, B. (2012). Five theses on understanding logistics as power. *Distinktion: Journal of Social Theory, 13*(3), 322–339. https://doi.org/10.1080/1600910X.2012.728533

New Zealand Flour Millers Association. (2020). Coronavirus: Foodstuffs sells 500 tonnes of extra flour during Covid-19 lockdown. Retrieved August 18, 2020, from https://flourinfo.co.nz/articles/coronavirus-foodstuffs-sells-1500-tonnes-extra-flour-during-covid-19-lockdown

NZ Pork. (2020). *New Zealand pork industry board annual report 2020*. NZ Pork.
Rae, S. (2020, July 27). Pork surplus crisis averted by measures. *Otago Daily Times*.
Standaert, M. (2020, May 27). 'Unstoppable': African swine fever deaths to eclipse record 2019 toll. *The Guardian*. https://www.theguardian.com/environment/2020/may/27/unstoppable-african-swine-fever-deaths-to-eclipse-record-2019-toll

CHAPTER 8

Reproducing Hunger in Pandemic America

Maggie Dickinson

Abstract The COVID-19 pandemic has precipitated a significant rise in hunger in the United States, especially among caretakers of children, people who are unemployed or insecurely employed, undocumented immigrants and other racialized marginalized groups. The gaping holes in the public response to growing hunger are the inevitable result of decades of welfare state transformation in which policymakers have withdrawn assistance for caregivers and reframed public benefits as a subsidy to low-wage jobs. In the face of mass unemployment and life-threatening risks for frontline food workers, hunger is once again being deployed as a tool to push people into unsafe jobs that prop up a racist and ecologically destructive food system.

Keywords Food insecurity • Social reproduction • Welfare policy • Racism

M. Dickinson (✉)
Department of Liberal Arts, Guttman Community College, CUNY,
New York, NY, USA
e-mail: Maggie.dickinson@guttman.cuny.edu

V. Stead, M. Hinkson (eds.), *Beyond Global Food Supply Chains*,
https://doi.org/10.1007/978-981-19-3155-0_8

One of the many ways the economic fallout from the pandemic has become legible to the public eye in the United States is through the rising visibility of hunger and food assistance. Early on, images of cars lined up for miles to collect food from food banks captured public attention. Demand at food banks across the country has been unrelenting. In October 2020, distributions from the not-for-profit organization Feeding America's network of food banks and pantries were up by 52 per cent on the monthly average before the pandemic. This increase does not include the contributions of the mutual aid groups that sprang up in communities across the United States to get food to elderly people, immune-compromised people and those otherwise in need. According to the Center on Budget and Policy Priorities, the available data suggest that between 6 and 7 million more people applied and were approved for SNAP (food stamp) benefits in the first six months of the pandemic. This rise is unprecedented: at the onset of the Global Financial Crisis of 2007–2008, it took nearly a year and a half to add this number of people to SNAP. This outpouring of pandemic-related food assistance has stemmed the tide of increasing food insecurity. Overall, food insecurity rates held steady in 2020 at 10.5 per cent of the US population, thanks to the expansion of both food and cash assistance (Coleman-Jensen et al., 2021).

However, like so many aspects of the pandemic, not all residents experienced the economic fallout in the same way. Reporters and commentators celebrated the "good news" that government intervention kept food insecurity levels stable during the economic upheaval of the pandemic. But as Ashanté Reese points out, a closer look at the data exposes the role racism plays in determining who goes hungry in the United States (Reese, 2021). Prior to the pandemic, Black and Latinx households were more likely to experience food insufficiency than white residents. The fallout from the pandemic and the response to it exacerbated these disparities. Even with the increase in food assistance, levels of food insecurity for Black households increased from 19.1 per cent in 2019 to 21.7 per cent in 2020, while food insecurity rates for white residents fell from 3.3 per cent in 2019 to 3 per cent in 2020 (Coleman-Jensen et al., 2021). In this racially segregated country, hunger can be mapped geographically. The most acute need is in areas where the majority of residents are Black or Native American. Black residents living in the South saw a greater increase in food insecurity in 2020 than other regions of the country (Coleman-Jensen et al., 2021). Of the top 25 counties with the highest projected food insecurity rates, only four—all in Kentucky—are majority white (Strochlic, 2020).

The experience of food insecurity in the United States is also conditioned by gender. The people tasked with the socially reproductive labour of caring for and raising children are structurally more vulnerable to hunger. Households with children saw an increase in food insecurity in 2020 from 13.6 per cent to 14.8 per cent. Single mothers of children were hardest hit, with 27.7 per cent of these families experiencing food insecurity in 2020 (Coleman-Jensen et al., 2021).

And yet none of this is new—even before the pandemic, hunger was an intractable problem in the United States, despite a massive expansion of food assistance in the twenty-first century. Nearly 40 million Americans received SNAP in 2019. The level of distribution of food-stamp rolls never really fell after the Global Financial Crisis began. Significantly, the vast majority of non-disabled, working-age adults on the SNAP rolls were employed. Soaring unemployment has exacerbated food insecurity in the United States, but having a job was hardly a solution to hunger before the pandemic—in 2019, unemployment was at its lowest rate in generations, yet 46 million people were sourcing food from a food bank. Despite a vast, growing food safety net that has continually expanded through the twenty-first century, 35 million people in the United States were food insecure in 2019. What is now clear is that more food assistance has not led to less hunger. Furthermore, the food crisis associated with the pandemic is a continuation of pre-pandemic hunger politics in the United States.

This gets us to the crux of the matter: hunger and poverty are permanent features of capitalist society—even in so-called good economic times. Our systems for preventing hunger are intentionally fragile and have emerged from a set of contradictory social forces. Our food safety net is massive, complex and not up to the task of making sure everyone who lives in the United States has enough to eat.

Work attachment and enforcement are the guiding ethos behind the current configuration of the US welfare state, and they are also at the heart of the utter failure to prevent a spiralling hunger crisis during the pandemic, particularly in communities of colour and among women caring for children. There has been tremendous resistance to maintaining supplementary unemployment payments and general cash payments because employers were concerned that people might refuse jobs (and get in the way of profit making). However, one form of assistance has been swift, generous and uncontroversial and that is charitable food assistance. This is the other aspect of the food safety net that we need to think about.

Charitable Food

Often called emergency food providers, soup kitchens and food pantries have evolved to become a permanent feature of the sprawling food safety net in the United States. These seemingly voluntary efforts have been summoned into being by federal funding over the last 40 years. Prior to the passage of The Emergency Food Assistance Program (TEFAP) in the early 1980s, food banks were small, rare, shoestring operations. Federal funding gave communities an incentive to establish food banks. And it was a very successful incentive. In 1979, there were 30 emergency food providers across New York City. Today there are over 1100. From March 2020 until the election of the Biden administration, the federal government dedicated $4.5 billion to emergency food providers while refusing to increase the value of SNAP or—better yet—provide people with sufficient cash assistance to enable them to stay home in order to help contain the pandemic. These public–private partnerships are staffed by volunteers—typically women—who do the hard work of keeping their communities fed. But the institutions operate primarily as sites for absorbing agricultural surplus and corporate food waste. Charitable food has become a safety valve for large agri-food industries, where overproduction and waste are part of the business model. These efforts also cheaply provide food for the most excluded, such as undocumented immigrants who are structurally barred from accessing social programmes and are particularly vulnerable to economic exploitation due to their legal status, and informally employed or unemployed people who cannot access wage supports.

Rather than employers absorbing the costs of social reproduction by offering time off, decent wages and flexibility for caretakers, or the state providing a social wage, either through direct cash support or expanded public services, the state offers economically insecure people food assistance. This assistance is geared towards staving off the worst effects of an exploitative capitalist system that demands more paid and unpaid labour from poor people, including engaging in time-consuming efforts to meet their basic needs, like waiting in long lines for food boxes (Elliott et al., 2021). As the working class absorbs these costs associated with social reproduction, wealth continues to accrue to the very richest in our society.

Our food safety net is entirely compatible with systems of capitalist accumulation, and that is why food assistance has become one of the go-to solutions to increased poverty and insecurity. It is the most thinkable solution because it is being used to grease the wheels of labour exploitation, not only by cutting assistance to poor families but also by effectively subsidizing low-wage work and encouraging community organizations to take responsibility for poverty and hunger by raising an army of voluntary labour to repurpose agribusiness food waste (Dickinson, 2020).

Social Reproduction and the Devaluation of Labour

The speed-up that women experienced during the pandemic, continuing to absorb socially reproductive labour alongside the push into low-paid employment, captures the unitary nature of the contemporary capitalist system. In a capitalist economy, there is a tendency for the wage relationship to shape all other relationships, including relations between spouses, children, parents, extended families and fictive kin. The labour associated with life-making, life-sustaining work in the home—such as caring for children, making meals, grocery shopping—are typically obscured through the ideology of the private family and the dogma of personal responsibility (Fraser, 2016). The situation many women and caretakers found themselves in during the pandemic—caught between a collapsing labour market, the demands of caring for children and a system of social supports that fails to adequately provide for people's basic needs—was simply an intensification of the pre-pandemic conditions they had endured. The federal government's absolute refusal to provide people with supports, such as regular cash payments and rent cancellation, and its bowing to pressure to keep the economy running by forcing people back to work despite an out-of-control, deadly virus have exposed the conditions low-income caretakers have been living with for a very long time, both in the home and in the workplace. The commitment to work enforcement on the part of the state in the face of the pandemic has intensified a long-standing hunger crisis for the racialized groups who have disproportionately struggled with food insecurity for decades.

The disproportionate impact of hunger on women with children, and on Black and Latinx households is unsurprising given the ways the pandemic has decimated the sectors of the economy dominated by these groups. Job losses have been concentrated in low-wage sectors such as leisure and hospitality, education and health services, and retail. Employers cut 140,000 jobs in December 2020. Stunningly, women accounted for all the job losses, losing 156,000 jobs, while men gained 16,000. Another survey found that Black women and Latinas lost jobs in December, while white women made significant gains. The instability and insecurity of the low-wage labour market has only become more insecure and unstable, as job losses have been concentrated in low-wage industries.

Food workers are some of the lowest-paid, least secure workers in the economy. They are more likely than workers in any other industry to rely on public benefits like SNAP because their wages are so low. In large part, this is because work that makes life possible, such as growing and cooking food, has long been relegated to women and racialized groups of people—from immigrants working in the fields, and enslaved people before them, to domestic workers and restaurant staff. These workers, viewed as cheap and disposable before the crisis, are now deemed essential—which, as others have noted, really means they are being treated as sacrificial (Gidla, 2020). They are being asked to risk their lives for paltry wages and with few protections so that the rest of the community can eat. Food workers are making terrible choices between going to work and risking illness or quitting the job that pays the bills and puts food on the table. A Long Beach grocery-store worker, profiled in an article on grocery chains closing stores in order to avoid paying locally mandated pay increases for these frontline workers, was quoted as saying she considered quitting out of fear of the virus but ultimately realized it was impossible because "I needed the money" (Bravo, 2021).

One study found that working-age adults in California had a 22 per cent increased risk of dying. But for agriculture and restaurant workers, that risk doubled to 40 per cent and for Latinx workers in those industries it was 60 per cent. In the food sector, restaurant and agricultural workers have been hit hardest, but warehouse, delivery, grocery and retail workers are also dying at higher rates (Chen et al., 2021). Outbreaks of coronavirus have been concentrated in meat-packing plants, as plant owners have lobbied the federal government to absolve them of any liability when workers fall ill or die due to conditions in these plants. Of course, the families of food workers are also at higher risk. Only 13 states have included frontline food workers in the first wave of people eligible for the vaccine. In the face of mass unemployment and life-threatening risks for frontline food workers, hunger is once again being used as a tool to prod the people who do this life-sustaining work into unsafe jobs. Work enforcement politics—which dominates our approach to hunger and poverty in the United

States—is aimed at making sure that the only way people can get money is by working for wages (Peck, 2001). This political commitment has turned the emergence of a dangerous novel virus into a protracted catastrophe on multiple fronts, including an escalating hunger crisis.

There is more than enough food for everyone living in the United States today—we throw away 30-40 per cent of the food we produce. People go hungry because they cannot lay claim to the food that exists. Most often, it is because they are un- or underemployed or their pay is too low (Dickinson, 2020). SNAP benefits help, but they are based on the thrifty food plan and do not provide enough to cover the costs of an entire month's worth of food. Most people run out of food stamps by the second or third week of the month. Food banks do what they can, but they are not designed to fulfil people's entire food needs either. The efforts made to get food to people in this moment are important, but they are not enough, because the food safety net is designed to manage a racialized labour force, not to decisively end hunger.

Cultivating Callousness

What the pandemic has unmasked is the centrality of death to the functioning of capitalism. The push to keep the economy open in the United States has clearly demonstrated that our economic system is premised on putting some people in danger and accepting their deaths as the price of doing business. We knew that opening restaurants and bars, and keeping meat-processing plants pumping out supply with no protections, meant that some of the people doing that work would die (Douglas, 2020). The prevalence of food insecurity among these same groups, racialized workers engaged in life-making labour, is part and parcel of an extractive economic system dependent on the vulnerability of food workers.

The fact that capitalism produces excess and unnecessary death is not new. Ruth Wilson Gilmore's definition of racism as "the state sanctioned or extralegal production and exploitation of group-differentiated vulnerability to premature death" is useful here (Gilmore, 2007). But the exposure to premature death is typically only visible to those directly affected by it—people who can see, every day, the physical, mental and emotional costs of a labour system that hastens death. For people higher up the income scale, and for policymakers in particular, these impacts often remain inchoate, subject to the need for investigation, requiring data and statistical picturing to confirm the truth of the matter. These techniques allow both callousness and indifference to flourish.

What have also been revealed are instances of concrete attempts to cultivate callousness about these inevitable deaths, particularly as the toll mounted. White supremacist small-business owners storming state capitols demanding an end to public health restrictions left no mystery as to the risks they were willing to take with their employees' lives. We were all asked to not care as policymakers refused to extend supplementary unemployment benefits in an attempt to force people back to work as the pandemic raged on.

There was a heightening of the contradictions under these circumstances. All of the reliable tropes that typically inure us to violence and death—whether fast or slow, structural or more immediate—didn't work in the same way in the face of a global pandemic. Characterizations of people as criminal or lazy that have been deployed to justify repressive policies from police murders to welfare reforms fell away in the face of the very real health risks we were all experiencing. Rather, we were confronted with the risks others were asked to take each time we ventured out to the grocery store.

In the absence of well-worn racialized tropes justifying why people needed to be disciplined into waged labour, we saw a rise in consciousness around the relative value of people's lives and well-being under an exploitative capitalist system. There was a countervailing rise in disgust at the naked appeals to accept preventable death as the price of doing business. There was a rejection of callousness, as there often is when economic pain is understood as occurring through no fault of your own (Dauber, 2013). We are beginning to see the fruits of this countervailing rejection of callousness. From the uprisings in summer 2020 that demanded recognition that Black lives matter to the resistance of workers refusing to return to exploitative, dangerous and unforgiving low-wage jobs, we are seeing an emergent consciousness around the value of life and life-making. How these nascent shifts in consciousness might shape the politics of hunger remains to be seen.

References

Bravo, K. (Producer). (2021, February 3). *Long Beach workers rally over planned closure of Food 4 Less, Ralph's blamed on city's hazard pay mandate*. KTLA.

Chen, Y.-H., Glymour, M., Riley, A., Balmes, J., Duchowny, K., Harrison, R., & Bibbins-Domingo, K. (2021). Excess mortality associated with the COVID-19 pandemic among Californians 18–65 years of age, by occupational sector and occupation: March through November 2020. *PLoS One, 16*(6), e0252454.

Coleman-Jensen, A., Rabbitt, M., Gregory, C., & Singh, A. (2021). *Economic research report No. 298: Household Food Security in the United States in 2020.* Economic Research Service, US Department of Agriculture. https://www.ers.usda.gov/publications/pub-details/?pubid=102075

Dauber, M. L. (2013). *The sympathetic state: Disaster relief and the origins of the American welfare state.* University of Chicago Press.

Dickinson, M. (2020). *Feeding the crisis: Care and abandonment in America's food safety net.* University of California Press.

Douglas, L. (2020, April 22). *Mapping covid-19 outbreaks in the food system.* Food and Environment Reporting Network. https://thefern.org/2020/04/mapping-covid-19-in-meat-and-food-processing-plants/

Elliott, S., Satterfield, S., Bowen, S., Hardison-Moody, A., & Williams, L. (2021). Disenfranchised: How lower income mothers navigated the social safety net during the COVID-19 pandemic. *Socius, 7.*

Fraser, N. (2016, July–August). Contradictions of capital and care. *New Left Review, 100.*

Gidla, S. (2020, May 5). We are not essential. We are sacrificial. *The New York Times.*

Gilmore, R. W. (2007). *Golden gulag: Prisons, surplus, crisis and opposition in globalizing California.* University of California Press.

Peck, J. (2001). *Workfare states.* Guilford Press.

Reese, A. (2021, October 7). The pandemic didn't "end hunger"—It exposed systemic racism instead. *Civil Eats.* https://civileats.com/2021/10/07/op-ed-the-pandemic-didnt-end-hunger-it-exposed-systemic-racism-instead/

Strochlic, N. (2020, November 25). *One in six Americans could go hungry in 2020 as pandemic persists.* National Geographic. Graphics by Riley D. Champine, Irene Berman-Vaporis, and Lawson Parker. https://www.nationalgeographic.com/history/article/one-in-six-could-go-hungry-2020-as-covid-19-persists#close

CHAPTER 9

The Pandemic Supermarket

David Boarder Giles

Abstract During the COVID-19 pandemic, this chapter argues, the supermarket became one of the most important sites in which the conditions and contradictions of capitalist food chains, laid bare by the crisis, were worked through, normalized and sustained. If supermarkets and grocery stores represent the archetypal endpoint of the value chain for commercial food systems—the interface between customer and commodity, where its value is realized—the social reproduction of this cultural logic in the face of unsettled circuits of production and consumption is indeed "essential" labour. But it is essential for deeper reasons than those highlighted in public discourse. This chapter describes the labours of employees and owners in a single independent grocery store in the Melbourne Central Business District over 18 months of lockdown, recession, and personal and economic uncertainty. It captures some of the innovations, improvisations and expressions of solidarity made both possible and necessary in the anticipation of an eventual return to "business as usual". These experiences throw into relief the supermarket's function as a definitive node that articulates the supply chains, consumer publics and regimes of precarious migrant labour that constitute the urban food system as a domain for the expropriation, circulation and accumulation of surplus value.

D. B. Giles (✉)
Deakin University, Melbourne, VIC, Australia
e-mail: d.giles@deakin.edu.au

V. Stead, M. Hinkson (eds.), *Beyond Global Food Supply Chains*,
https://doi.org/10.1007/978-981-19-3155-0_9

Keywords COVID-19 • Grocery workers • Essential labour • Affective labour • Social reproduction • Commodification

The Spectacle of Scarcity

"I started just around when COVID was starting to hit", Girish told me. Originally from Nepal, he studies accounting and works at my local supermarket in the Melbourne Central Business District (CBD). He's been there since March 2020. "My first thought was, 'one or two months and this will be gone'", he said. That was 18 months ago. I've gotten to know Girish and his coworkers quite well since then. For weeks on end, they were some of the only three-dimensional faces I saw when I left my apartment for one of the four reasons permitted under Victoria's stage-four lockdown: buying groceries. Below, I digest their impressions of the pandemic.

"It was funny", Girish told me, "I had like an intuition, one day. I was just about to come to work, and the weather was a bit dark and gloomy. Weather like a scene from a movie. And I told my brother-in-law, 'This is weird … I think something is going to happen'. And I came to work that day. And I think after two to three days of that, we went to lockdown". He's not alone in trawling the filmic imaginary to render a crisis intelligible when more quotidian vernaculars fail to furnish working heuristics. As in disasters of the past, before official or collective responses had congealed, the interruption of social, economic and political life was framed in the popular imagination by familiar stock narratives of scarcity (see Beaumont, 2014; Kierner, 2019). Thus, inchoate existential uncertainties gave way to culturally coded panic, with corresponding consumer tactics: *people stocked up*.

Ubiquitous toilet paper shortages were the tip of the iceberg. "We had run three counters there", Girish told me of the panic buying that characterized the first few weeks of the initial lockdown. "All our counters were busy—like [with] three people working the counter, our lines extended back to the back door … Every counter, all the lines were to the back of the door. And it did seem like a scene from a movie. Like, people holding toilet paper, and pasta, and canned food, and chips and stuff … like this thing is really happening. People are doing it." The spectacle of long lines and bare shelves itself became a trope rehearsed in the nightly news, a recursive semiotic (news-imitates-life-imitates-disaster-fiction) with which to make sense of the early days of the crisis. "As soon as the lockdown started", Girish told me, "what you heard around the news, that was happening in our store. People were really clambering about toilet paper. After that, two to three days later, we started putting on the limits on our things. Like pasta—two packs of pasta and one toilet paper, per transaction".

In these moments, the familiar forum of the supermarket became a cipher for the opaque alterity of the coronavirus pandemic (both the epidemiological phenomenon and the corresponding sociocultural, political and economic event). Evacuated shelves and panicked consumers became the imaginative landscape within which the crisis was worked through. In this chapter, I argue that supermarkets and grocery stores became a critical site of social reproduction, where anxieties about the virus and deeper political and economic tensions were rehearsed, regulated or resolved. The labour by which this was accomplished was surely "essential" labour but essential for deeper reasons than those typically highlighted in public discourse; it was deployed in the social reproduction of capitalist relationships of labour and consumption (Stevano et al., 2021; see also Bhattacharya, 2017).

Perhaps even more than other retailers, supermarkets trade in a sensorium of abundance, predictability and mundane domesticity. They represent a cornerstone of the household imaginary, the consumer oikos that is one of the fundamental social units that organize capitalist social relations (Cooper, 2019). Grocers and other food retailers therefore lean heavily on visual signifiers of bounty and affluence to encourage consumption; full shelves are prioritized to inspire consumer confidence and desire—even if much of that food goes unsold (Stuart, 2009, p. 27). In this way, they are a simulacrum of the surfeit of the consumer with the global market at their fingertips.

But for the same reason, they are haunted by hunger. The empty shelf repels customers (Stuart, 2009, p. 17), emanating a horror vacui that taps into latent awareness of the scarcity manufactured by capitalist value chains. Customers intuit that markets do not distribute resources efficiently according to need and that food and shelter are wasted in the face of food and housing insecurity (Springer, 2020). News media underscored this with images of food stocks destroyed by farmers and wholesalers during the pandemic due to labour shortages and interrupted supply chains—juxtaposed with long lines at foodbanks and welfare offices (see Dickinson, this volume). Although Australian authorities suggested otherwise, from a certain perspective, it was entirely rational to hoard food, toilet paper and other goods.

At the outset of the earliest lockdowns, this incipient consumer panic became a self-fulfilling prospect. Stocks that usually would have lasted for two to three weeks lasted for two to three days. "As soon as the lockdown hit", Girish told me, "we were out of everything". The pandemic instantly revealed both the vulnerability and the obscurity of our supply chains.

In this context, the pandemic supermarket served a more specific function than the mere satisfaction of sustenance—which, after all, has been accomplished in myriad ways during moments of both acute and long-term capitalist crisis, from May 1968's rural–urban cooperatives to the ever-growing foodbanks of the contemporary charitable sector, or indeed grassroots mutual aid networks serving, especially vulnerable individuals under lockdown. In contrast, the pandemic supermarket maintained the logic of capitalist production and distribution. The job of grocery clerks like Girish, therefore—from the performance of reassurance and normalcy to the enforcement of social distance—worked with and within the economic and social shocks of the pandemic to recuperate them under the organizing principles of a consumer oikos.

The Paradigmatic Commodity Context

The supermarket is one of the quintessential mechanisms by which the commodity form is normalized and sustained with respect to the food system. Supermarkets and grocery stores, perhaps more than any other retailer, represent the archetypal endpoint of the value chain for our commercial food systems—the interface between customer and commodity, where its value is worked through. They instantiate a paradigmatic "commodity context", as Arjun Appadurai might have called it (1986), wherein the product is apprehended qua product and its value realized. They therefore reinscribe the food commodity as a fetish—obscuring the conditions of its production and distribution that confer value upon it (Dixon et al., 2014). Yet in this way, supermarkets also represent a cipher for the entire chain (see also Giles, 2016, 2021). They are its fundamental horizon and compass point.

As Wolfgang Fritz Haug (1986) reminds us, no commodity's value is ever certain. He builds on Marx's insight that capitalist value is a kind of "social hieroglyphic" (2000 [1865], p. 475), a subjective expression of the social relationships of production, distribution and consumption that propel commodities into circulation. As such, that value remains fungible and unrealized right up until the point of sale, where it performs its "salto mortale" (Haug, 1986, p. 23), the death-defying leap from virtual to concrete. This leap cannot occur in a vacuum, of course. Haug suggests that its trajectory is defined by contexts and pathways of commodity aesthetics—such as those created by retail environments. In other words, its value is reckoned at each turn through affective and aesthetic judgements, in a cultural context where those judgements are rendered sensible (in both senses of the word). His insight helps us to begin to think about what kind of place a supermarket is.

Haug was writing in the 1970s, at an inflexion point, when the variety and volume of supermarket offerings was beginning to grow remarkably in industrialized nations (Goldfrank, 2005), corresponding to growth in both consumer and commercial food waste (Rathje & Murphy, 1992; Stuart, 2009). In many ways, the subsequent decades have been a period in which the commodity's value has been increasingly driven by such affective determinations, although not limited to aesthetics narrowly understood. The post-Fordist era, as theorists like Antonio Negri (1992) and Maurizio Lazzarato (2006) have argued, has been one defined not solely or even primarily by the industrial labour of producing goods per se but by the "immaterial labour" (or "biopolitical production", if you prefer their alternative formulation) of remaking social relationships of all kinds, all in the service of remaking our relationship to goods themselves. Indeed, according to Lazzarato, the postmodern commodity is an object primarily defined by information and affect. We can understand the supermarket, then, as a site of immaterial labour and biopolitical production par excellence, both congealing, rendering and making legible otherwise obscure supply chains and entangling our household rhythms with the commodity form, normalizing its part in our very sustenance. In other words, it is not the labour of producing that material use value that will be bought and sold for a price but rather the labour reproducing the mechanism by which exchange values (specifically) and exchange value (in general) are realized.

And in the face of crisis—or indeed, crises, as the pandemic revealed and provoked countless underlying contradictions and instabilities, both specifically in the food system and in late capitalism at large—as a commodity context, cipher and horizon for late-capitalist food chains, the supermarket and its immaterial, affective labours also served to restabilize the food commodity form in the face of pandemic shocks to the system.

In this context, the pandemic threatened the fates of business owners, grocery workers and commodities themselves with parallel forms of abandonment or abjection, as food lingered overlong on the shelves, employees lived in increasing uncertainty regarding visas and employment pathways, and owners hung anxiously on the sparse traffic of shoppers that kept them from going under. In their everyday biopolitical labours, these stakeholders instantiated such entangled urban circuits of value and looming dereliction. Their innovations, improvisations and expressions of solidarity were made both possible and necessary in the anticipation of a "return to normal". Those adaptations and normalizations—by which some novel version of business-as-usual was established—are the stuff of immaterial and affective labour. Such labour was essential to the maintenance of the supermarket as an ongoing matrix for the realization of the food commodity form.

Obscure Supply Chains and Inscrutable Demand

Obscure supply chains and inscrutable demand characterized much of the pandemic for my interlocutors at the supermarket. By definition, of course, the introduction of a pathogen that avails itself of human connectivity disrupts relationships across the social fabric, including those relationships of production, distribution and consumption for which the supermarket is a translation matrix. In the process, however, the pandemic revealed how opaque or ineffable those relationships had often been.

For example, while the initial avalanche of sales was the most spectacular, headline-grabbing consequence of the pandemic for the grocery retailers, the more enduring implication—at least for the store in question—was the attrition of sales afterwards. Within a week or two of panic buying, demand dried up. Under Victoria's stage-four restrictions, the store saw up to a 60 per cent drop in receipts. Even months after the end of Melbourne's longest, 112-day lockdown, and a putative return to "normal" during the city's relatively long period of relaxed restrictions in early 2021, with fewer people working in CBD offices and fewer attractions to draw them back, sales had fallen far short of pre-pandemic rates. "Our bosses thought that demand would be high", said another clerk, Thapa, describing initial attempts to stock the store, "but they were wrong".

Of course, the experience of distinct kinds of supermarkets in different locales varied widely, with some noting reduced patronage as customers avoided leaving the house (Castelló & Casasnovas, 2020), while others (especially those offering delivery services) recorded greater sales as customers stayed and ate at home (Stewart & Stewart, 2020; Troy, 2021). However, the unevenness of the transformation of commercial food chains is precisely part of the point. Even under relaxed restrictions and a partial "return to normal", for the CBD supermarket in question, demand remained less predictable—not only in scale but in kind. As Naresh, who has worked there for three years, explained to me, they had to check the shelves more regularly to see what had and hadn't sold in a given period. Product waste was less predictable and more common as a result, employees told me.

Indeed, as widely reported elsewhere, each of the employees I spoke with told me waste was a fundamental feature of the pandemic disruptions at my local supermarket. Products typically never thrown away before, like soft drinks and chocolate bars, were wasted in great quantities early in Victoria's first lockdowns. The same pattern of waste was repeated, to a lesser degree, at the outset of the city's subsequent "snap" lockdowns. Some unsold items were retrieved and replaced by suppliers—a common element of the commercial compact between wholesaler and retailer. And much of the excess was donated to food recovery charities such as Second Bite, who fed people who might otherwise have been buying groceries from supermarkets before the crisis. Indeed, in this respect, the pandemic consolidated a growing trend towards the joint enclaving of both commercial food surpluses and economically surplus, or precarious, communities in marginal disciplinary spaces like food pantries—a joint distribution of wealth and waste (Giles, 2016). Additionally, some of the excesses went home with supermarket employees (some small compensation for their diminished hours). And a great deal of food was placed in the bin. Fresh produce was the major thing that needed to be thrown away, Naresh told me. And indeed, throughout the lockdown, the neglected, wilted and overripe produce I found on the store's shelves remain one of the most emblematic signifiers of the breakdown of market norms—a far cry from the aesthetics of abundance that characterized the typical pre-pandemic supermarket.

With stock that would previously have lasted a matter of days now sitting on the shelves for weeks, deliveries from the supermarket's parent company—also its primary supplier—were ratcheted down from every week to every three weeks. And while that supplier still delivers 90 per cent of the store's stock, according to Thapa, its supply chains were nonetheless disrupted in a range of ways. Thapa remembered, for example, the strange experience of trying to restock toilet paper following the initial panic and being delivered only a single pallet—much less than ordered. Throughout the first year of lockdown, there were other shortages of various products for reasons similarly inscrutable from the vantage point of the aisles—blueberries, raspberries or limes, for instance (the latter of which briefly tripled in price).

Maybe most telling was the long, anxious process of sourcing new stock when the existing suppliers failed. Girish told me about days on which his boss was up until two in the morning looking for new sources from which to order product. One of the owners himself told me that he'd been forced to devote time and effort to liaising in new ways with other retailers and restaurants across the CBD. Despite its putative role as the holistic prism through which value chains are refracted, when the usual, familiar channels are disrupted, those value chains turn out to be profoundly opaque, hidden from even the buyers—those agents who are ostensibly best placed to engage with and evaluate them.

This obscurity was captured perfectly—and not without some cheek—by Thapa, who told me about a conspiracy theory that had circulated among some of his friends to account for the toilet paper shortages. Since China produces a great deal of the country's toilet paper, they reasoned, Chinese authorities must be deliberately throttling down the world's supply for their own nefarious reasons. It's telling that this was a more concrete account of the supply chain than any other Thapa had at hand.

Essential Labour

In spite of these disjunctures, what struck me most about the day-to-day operations of the store was, simply, that they *went on*. The experience employees described was of arriving at a new normal, however temporary. This ersatz normality not only assimilated new biopolitical regulatory apparatuses, both directly (as when health agencies visited the store to ensure compliance) and indirectly (as when some customers began to object to employees touching their food), but also recalibrated and rearticulated new forms of market sociality, in order to allow the supermarket to continue to perform its primary function as the horizon of commercial food chains in pandemic flux.

If, as I have argued above, the supermarket is a site par excellence of immaterial, affective production—whose chief "product" is the hegemony of, and our own routinized relationship to, the edible commodity form—then the work of incorporating the pandemic into that relationship is an "essential" form of labour. Indeed, pandemic transformations of the food system *also* bolstered alternative forms of food distribution, yielding new markets for retail delivery models such as Amazon Fresh (Stewart & Stewart, 2020; Hobbs, 2020) and new grassroots mutual aid networks, deploying non-market care packages of food and other necessities (Sitrin & Sembrar, 2020). The pandemic therefore threw into relief the everyday affective and "phatic labour" (Elyachar, 2010) that reproduces the cultural-economic context of the supermarket (see also Tolich, 1993). What was most essential was its role in working through the pandemic within the commodity context of the supermarket and vice versa.

It is telling, for example, that—whereas I was perhaps expecting to encounter stories of exploitative hours or unpaid overtime under pandemic duress, along with hostility and disrespect from anxious customers, along with racist overtones, considering that the grocery workers I spoke with were all South Asian—what I heard were stories of gratitude and solidarity in the face of adversity. Employees spoke with deep relief of the owners' refusal to sack any staff, even those to whom "JobKeeper", the federal wage subsidy instituted during the first year of the pandemic, wasn't available due to their temporary-visa status (although hours were inevitably reduced as a result). And staff told me happily of customers' consistent, dutiful, respectful observance of new regulations such as social distancing and the wearing of face masks. The production of this convivial setting (however constrained by the mood of life under lockdown) was a crucial component of their work.

This essential labour is also *skilled labour*. Consider the work of commodity aesthetics for which each of the employees was responsible; in the face of sparse and sedentary shelf stock, the staff did what they could to approximate the sensory environment of the paradigmatic supermarket, rearranging goods to minimize bare shelves and reminding customers of their desirous relationship to the commodity. Further, considering the inescapable amount of waste described above, staff were obliged to do what I have elsewhere called the "work of waste-making"—the subjective valorization and devalorization of shelf stock that consigns some items to the bin in order to lend more currency to the remaining goods (Giles, 2021).

And in addition to being skilled, the work of reproducing the pandemic supermarket is *precarious* labour—often done for relatively low wages by people who are under pressure or vulnerable as a result of their status. Most staff were students on temporary visas. They are highly educated and correspondingly highly skilled, but only entitled to work a limited number of hours, not entitled to the JobKeeper wage subsidy, and living in ongoing uncertainty about their status and future in Australia.

The pressures were myriad. One colleague had returned to India permanently because he found life under these conditions unsustainable. Others anxiously searched for full-time employment, as their visa requirements had apparently recently changed. Others were separated from family, including a new child born in India after the borders closed. Others were forced to seek support from the Red Cross. These, too, are the costs of reproducing the pandemic supermarket—the material externalities of "immaterial" labour.

Indeed, some of my interlocutors were precisely the people Prime Minister Scott Morrison had expressly told to leave at the outset of the pandemic—and the point was not lost on them. As Naresh told me, "Australia has got a bad reputation from the time of COVID, how they have managed international students here. And obviously, the word of mouth spreads so fast … Because Scott Morrison said to just go home. You know, that has a direct impact on how people treat temporary residents here. You know what I mean? If a leader says, 'We're all in this together so we should be together', that would have changed the perspective of how we go about it". Naresh hastened to add that, in spite of being frontline workers, they were not afforded priority access to the vaccine in the way that healthcare and aged care workers were. To people like Morrison, Naresh is at the end of the food chain in more ways than one.

Conclusion

Capitalist food chains were, paradoxically, both unsettled and entrenched by COVID-19. And nowhere were pandemic foodways more simultaneously exceptional and quotidian than at the supermarket. Grocery stores represented a critical site of social reproduction, where the political-economic conditions and contradictions revealed by the crisis were worked through, reconciled or normalized—or at least bracketed and neutralized.

If supermarkets and grocery stores represent the archetypal endpoint of the value chain for commercial food systems—the interface between customer and commodity, where the commodity's value is realized—the social reproduction of this cultural logic in the face of unsettled circuits of production and consumption is essential labour. But it is essential for deeper reasons than those highlighted in public discourse about this emerging category of work. The efforts of employees and owners in a single independent grocery store in the Melbourne CBD over 18 months of lockdown, recession, and personal and economic uncertainty represent in microcosm the affective and phatic functions of this essential labour. They throw into relief the supermarket's role as a definitive node that articulates the supply chains, consumer publics and regimes of precarious migrant labour that constitute the urban food system as a domain for the expropriation, circulation and accumulation of surplus value. Their innovations, improvisations and expressions of solidarity were both possible and necessary in the anticipation of an imagined return to "business as usual". In the process, they renegotiated and remapped the unsettled landscape of urban food chains and maintained the integrity of the commodity context upon which so many of us relied to sustain ourselves.

References

Appadurai, A. (1986). Introduction: Commodities and the politics of value. In A. Appadurai (Ed.), *The social life of things: Commodities in Cultural Perspective*. Cambridge University Press.

Beaumont, M. (2014). Imagining the end times: Ideology, the contemporary disaster movie, *contagion*. In M. Flisfeder & L.-P. Willis (Eds.), *Žižek and Media Studies*. Palgrave.

Bhattacharya, T. (2017). Introduction: Mapping social reproduction theory. In T. Bhattacharya (Ed.), *Social reproduction theory: Remapping class, Recentering oppression*. Pluto Press.

Castelló, J. V., & Casasnovas, G. L. (2020). The effect of lockdowns and infection rates on supermarket sales. *Economics and Human Biology, 40*(8), 10.1016/j.ehb.2020.100947.

Cooper, M. (2019). *Family values: Between neoliberalism and the new social conservatism*. Zone Books.

Dixon, J., Hattersley, L., & Isaacs, B. (2014). Transgressing retail: Supermarkets, liminoid power and the metabolic rift. In M. Goodman & C. Sage (Eds.), *Food transgressions: Making sense of contemporary food politics*. Ashgate.

Elyachar, J. (2010). Phatic labor, infrastructure, and the question of empowerment in Cairo. *American Ethnologist, 37*(3), 452–464.

Giles, D. B. (2016). Distributions of wealth, distributions of waste: Abject capital and accumulation by disposal. In L. F. Angosto-Ferrández & G. H. Presterudstuen (Eds.), *Anthropologies of value*. Pluto Press.

Giles, D. B. (2021). *A mass conspiracy to feed people: Food not bombs and the world-class waste of global cities*. Duke University Press.
Goldfrank, W. L. (2005). Fresh demand: The consumption of Chilean produce in the United States. In J. L. Watson & M. Caldwell (Eds.), *The cultural politics of food and eating*. Blackwell Publishing.
Haug, W. F. (1986). *Critique of commodity aesthetics: Appearance, sexuality, and advertising in capitalist society*. University of Minnesota Press.
Hobbs, J. E. (2020). Food supply chains during the COVID-19 pandemic. *Canadian Journal of Agricultural Economics, 68*, 171–176.
Kierner, C. A. (2019). *Inventing disaster: The culture of calamity from the Jamestown Colony to the Johnstown flood*. University of North Carolina Press.
Lazzarato, M. (2006). Immaterial labor. In P. Virno & M. Hardt (Eds.), *Radical thought in Italy: A potential politics (theory out of bounds)*. University of Minnesota Press.
Marx, K. ([1865] 2000). Capital. In D. MacLellan (Ed.), *Selected writings*. Oxford University Press.
Negri, A. (1992). *Marx beyond Marx*. Pluto Press.
Rathje, W., & Murphy, C. (1992). *Rubbish: The anthropology of garbage*. Harper Collins.
Sitrin, M., & Sembrar, C. (2020). *Pandemic solidarity: Mutual aid during the Covid-19 crisis*. Pluto Press.
Springer, S. (2020, March 15). *Toilet paper wars and the shithouse of capitalism*. Common Dreams. https://www.commondreams.org/views/2020/03/15/toilet-paper-wars-and-shithouse-capitalism
Stevano, S., Ali, R., & Jamieson, M. (2021). Essential for what? A global social reproduction view on the re-organisation of work during the COVID-19 pandemic. *Canadian Journal of Development Studies, 42*(1–2), 178–199.
Stewart, B. L., & Stewart, J. F. (2020). Pandemic panic and retail reconfiguration: Consumer and supply chain responses to COVID-19. *Journal of Family & Consumer Sciences, 113*(1), 7–16.
Stuart, T. (2009). *Waste: Uncovering the global food scandal*. Penguin.
Tolich, M. B. (1993). Alienating and liberating emotions at work: Supermarket clerks' performance of customer service. *Journal of Contemporary Ethnography, 22*(3), 361–381.
Troy, M. (2021, May 18). *Pandemic-fueled record growth in 2020: The PG 100: An unprecedented year on many levels saw sales surge to new heights*. Progressive Grocer. https://progressivegrocer.com/pandemic-fueled-record-growth-2020-pg-100

PART IV

Food Politics

CHAPTER 10

Disruption as Reprieve?

Jon Altman and Francis Markham

Abstract It is a truism that the impacts of any crisis always fall unevenly. In this chapter, we focus on the experience of COVID-19 by a particular population group, Indigenous Australians living in extremely remote circumstances. Here key responses to the disruption wrought by the pandemic have paradoxically registered as reprieve. In Australia, remote-living Indigenous peoples live in deep poverty and were anticipated to be highly vulnerable to food insecurity and supply chain disruption. Surprisingly, the pandemic served to disrupt in other ways. The hegemonic characterization of welfare-dependent Indigenous peoples as morally deficient subjects in need of discipline and control could not be sustained as the country "locked down" and over a million others became "welfare dependent" overnight. Unemployment benefits were temporarily doubled, and onerous work-for-the-dole mutual obligations eased. This essay explores

J. Altman (✉)
School of Regulation and Global Governance, The Australian National University, Canberra, ACT, Australia
e-mail: jon.altman@anu.edu.au

F. Markham
Centre for Aboriginal Economic Policy Research (CAEPR), The Australian National University, Canberra, ACT, Australia
e-mail: francis.markham@anu.edu.au

V. Stead, M. Hinkson (eds.), *Beyond Global Food Supply Chains*,
https://doi.org/10.1007/978-981-19-3155-0_10

potential positive changes to systems of food provisioning caused by government responses to COVID-19. The remote food security "crisis" is shown to be mainly an artefact of government policies designed to punish the poor and push unemployed remote-community residents into jobs. We propose permanent reform to the social security system that will enhance food security and liberate Indigenous peoples to more effectively self-provision and exercise "food sovereignty".

Keywords Indigenous peoples • Indigenous food sovereignty • Indigenous food security • Remote stores • Supply chains • Welfare conditionality

Food Pricing and Security in Remote Indigenous Australia

When the COVID-19 pandemic arrived on Australian shores, measures were quickly enacted to protect the Indigenous residents of remote regions whose poor health status rendered them particularly vulnerable to the disease (Keene, 2020). In late March 2020, remote communities were declared restricted zones under the *Biosecurity Act* 2015 (Cth), with entry only allowed for those delivering essential services including food. In early April 2020, a Food Security Working Group was established by the Australian government. And then in May 2020, the Minister for Indigenous Australians established a parliamentary inquiry into food pricing and food security in remote Indigenous communities. We both provided submissions to this inquiry (Altman, 2020; Markham & Kerins, 2020). At the same time as these Indigenous-specific actions were being implemented, broader measures were introduced to bolster the livelihood circumstances of all Australians who were economically impacted by the lockdowns that have become an enduring feature of Australia's effort to manage the spread of the virus. Of relevance to this essay was the introduction of a coronavirus income supplement to all unemployed Australians, among whom Indigenous Australians are disproportionately represented. This one measure effectively doubled the income of 38 per cent of Indigenous people (Markham et al., 2020, p. 6). Further, with lockdown, mutual obligation "work for the dole" requirements were relaxed as a social-distancing measure. This was especially relevant for remote-living Indigenous Australians, as their income support was conditional on extremely onerous work-for-the-dole requirements, with harsh financial penalties for non-compliance (Staines et al., 2021, pp. 10–12).

In December 2020, the *Report Food Pricing and Food Security in Remote Indigenous Communities* (Commonwealth of Australia, 2020) was released. It found that food costs are very high in many remote communities, reinforcing long-held concerns regarding food security for Aboriginal and Torres Strait Islander peoples, many of whom live in deep poverty. Such concerns had been articulated by several government inquiries in the last decade (Fredericks & Bradfield, 2021) and had even been the subject of a now defunct National Strategy for Food Security in Remote Indigenous Communities, introduced by the Council of Australian Governments in 2009 as an element of its Closing the Gap policy framework. But the report found no evidence of systemic price-gouging taking place in remote community stores, nor of significant food shortages—concerns that had triggered the parliamentary inquiry. Optimistically the parliamentary committee noted the positive impacts of two new institutions, the Food Security Working Group and the Supermarket Taskforce, established in 2020 in response to the pandemic.

The report's 16 recommendations focused on technical and surveillance interventions that the committee expected would apply downward pressure on food prices at remote stores and ensure that healthy fresh foods were available. Only one recommendation referred to the need for locally sourced food, focusing on local commercial market gardens and animal husbandry rather than fishing and wild harvesting of bush foods, at which many Indigenous people are especially adept. There was no serious engagement by the parliamentary committee with two key issues that we raised in our submissions (two of 126 received), based on community-based research on economic well-being in remote Indigenous communities. First, given the workings of supply chain capitalism, food prices in remote stores inevitably will be high. The payment of the Coronavirus Supplement in 2020 provided a natural experiment on how the alleviation of deep poverty might enhance food security in a context where food prices are high. Second, institutional arrangements like mutual obligation limited opportunities for self-provisioning. The liberation of the unemployed from mutual-obligation requirements, combined with extra income, allowed some people to visit their customary lands and engage in self-provisioning. It is these two forms of livelihood and well-being reprieve during the early days of the pandemic disruption that we explore in this essay.

Long Supply Chain: Expensive Food and Low Incomes

Remote and very remote Australia as officially classified today accounts for 86 per cent of the Australian continent; this classification clearly demonstrates a dominant market-capitalist and settler-state perspective from the highly urbanized, densely settled parts of Australia. The dots on the map are discrete Indigenous communities, so termed for demographic (most residents are Indigenous) and historical (most of the larger places were colonial settlements; the small ones are more recently re-established homelands) reasons. There are about 1000 discrete Indigenous communities with a population of about 90,000–100,000 people (10 per cent non-Indigenous), serviced by 200 community stores. While most of the small communities have no store, a few of the larger ones have more than one. Much of this information is cartographically depicted in Fig. 10.1.

People in these communities live at the end of long distribution and, more importantly, fragile supply chains, whether their store food originates in Australia or overseas. It is inevitable that 1000 discrete Indigenous communities in tropical and desert Australia will experience supply chain challenges. Indeed, it is remarkable that fresh and processed foods routinely reach these extraordinarily remote places by road, sea and air delivery, especially when the rugged terrain and extreme seasonality and associated periodic isolation of many places are considered.

The small size of communities eliminates access to supermarket chains and oligopoly wholesale outlets. Inevitably, food supply comes at a high price, something that has been recognized and clearly documented for decades now, most regularly by the Northern Territory Market Basket Survey, conducted every two years for the past two decades. Small markets and limited buying power, lack of retail competition, high freight and associated cool-storage costs all add up: that is the way market capitalism works. Numerous reviews that we refer to in our submissions indicate that a "healthy" food basket costs 20–60 per cent more in remote Indigenous situations and 60–68 per cent more using point-of-sale data at 20 remote stores.

One broad response to this situation is to reduce the cost of store-purchased food, as in the parliamentary committee's recommendations, which look to lower prices through price monitoring, infrastructure improvements and other technical interventions into store and supply chain management. This mirrors the approach generally taken in the public health literature on food-security interventions. The other, which we

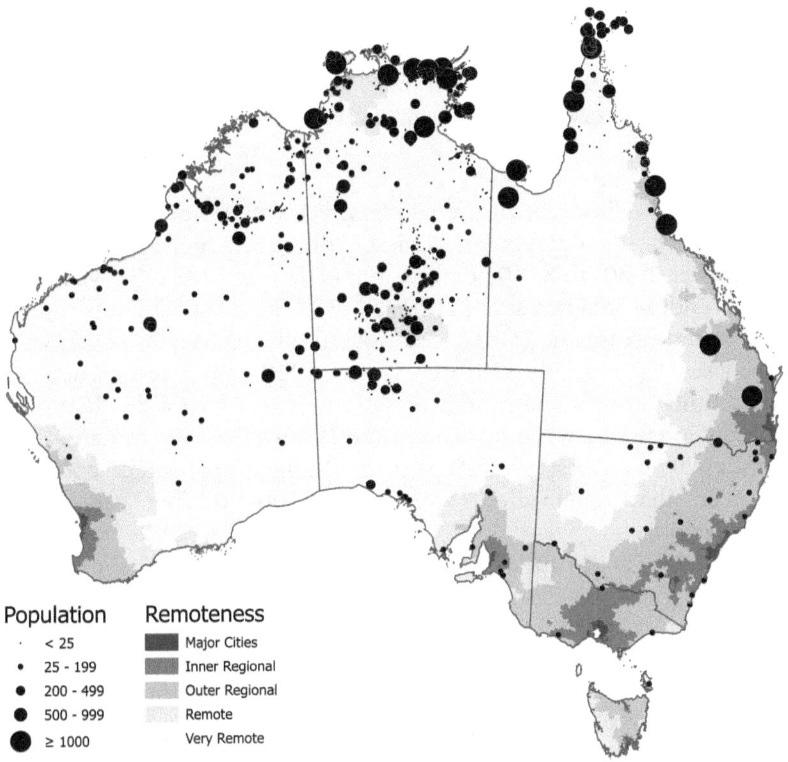

Fig. 10.1 Discrete Indigenous communities in remote Australia

favour, is to raise cash income levels in remote communities to allow for the purchase of food at what are inevitably higher prices.

Most Indigenous people in very remote Australia (53 per cent) live below the poverty line (Markham & Biddle, 2018). This rate has increased significantly between 2006 and 2016. This is partly explained by an increase in Indigenous unemployment: in very remote Australia the Indigenous employment rate declined from nearly 50 per cent to 30 per cent between 2006 and 2016; it is the lowest in the country. The prevalence of remote Indigenous poverty is the single greatest contributor to food insecurity. The Australian Bureau of Statistics *National Aboriginal and Torres Strait Islander Health Survey* (ABS, 2019) asked participants if they ran out of food and were unable to buy more in the past twelve months. In very remote Australia, 43 per cent of Indigenous people reported experiencing such food insecurity in 2018–2019. In a submission to another parliamentary inquiry and using the best available epidemiological evidence, we noted that a combination of low income, limited choice and high food prices is literally killing Indigenous Australians (Markham & Altman, 2019).

During the first year of the pandemic, as a series of supplements were paid to the unemployed, declining from $550 per fortnight (April–September 2020) to $150 per fortnight (1 January 2021–31 March 2021) before ending (Staines et al., 2021, p. 13). These supplements resulted in dramatic decreases in Indigenous poverty and markedly enhanced food purchases. For example, Outback Stores (2020), a publicly owned remote community store management corporation, reported a 75–100 per cent increase in sales between April and June 2020. The Arnhem Land Progress Aboriginal Corporation (2020), an Indigenous-owned corporation, reported that retail sales increased by 200–300 per cent over the same period.

The COVID disruption provided a rare form of social experimentation that is only possible during exceptional times. The raising of incomes for all by as much as 26 per cent not only offset the high price of purchased food for a time but simultaneously allowed Australia to start to address its international commitments to eliminate poverty and hunger by 2030 in accord with Sustainable Development Goals 1 and 2 of the UN Global 2030 Agenda for Sustainable Development.

There are two starkly contrasting views here. The parliamentary inquiry focused on issues of competition and price monitoring, transport and refrigeration infrastructure, and store regulation and monitoring. In short, the inquiry's considered view of poverty and hunger in remote Indigenous communities exhibited a concentrated technical focus on the supply chain. We, on the other hand, use information from the COVID income-supplementation period to highlight the inadequacy of social-security payments that include a Remote Area Allowance that still fails to reflect the higher cost of living in remote Australia. After a six-month period of the gradual tapering down of the COVID supplement, the JobSeeker rate was increased by only $50 per fortnight from 1 April 2021. The experiment of poverty alleviation is now over, and the majority of remote-living Indigenous Australians have now returned to a life of food insecurity, living at the end of the global food supply chain.

Short Supply Chains: Self-Provisioning

In precolonial times, Indigenous people everywhere in Australia exercised food sovereignty and enjoyed diverse forms of self-sufficiency by utilizing the natural environment and its resources. This mode of production was disrupted by colonization, dispossession and settler-state domination that only occurred in some of the remotest parts of the continent after the Second World War. The transformation from self-provisioning societies to the income poverty and high levels of dependence on store-bought foods evident today involved extremely complex processes: we can explore such processes in only a cursory manner here.

There is limited empirical information about the extent of Indigenous people's self-provisioning across the more than 6 million square kilometres of Australia we now term remote and very remote. The information that is available and summarized by Buchanan (2014) and Ferguson et al. (2017) indicates that contemporary self-provisioning occurs at varying levels of significance. Statistics from the National Aboriginal and Torres Strait Islander Social Survey that we summarized (Altman, 2020; Markham & Kerins, 2020) indicate that between 72 per cent of adults in remote Australia in 2008 and 79 per cent in 2014 reported participation in some hunting, fishing, and gathering of wild foods. While the survey data on participation is far from comprehensive, it is unlikely that such high levels of effort were undertaken without reward.

Despite the numbers, there is an escalating government project to impose a market mentality on remote-living Indigenous people. This project is ideologically underpinned by what Martin and Yanagisako (2020) have identified as a modernist teleological vision of a future in which wage labour would expand across the world. Hence, the coercive policy of punitive workfare for the unemployed aims to prepare them for paid employment even in situations where employment opportunities are deficient or absent, and labour migration is not countenanced as an option by most unemployed.

To challenge and potentially upend the dominant discourse promoting market capitalism as the only means for poverty alleviation and food security in remote Australia, we propose an alternate Indigenous perspective: hunting and harvesting of naturally occurring foods as a form of self-provisioning, sometimes referred to as food sovereignty. Our proposal is not for some return to pre-colonial subsistence living but rather for an enhancement of livelihoods, especially for the unemployed, who might be well placed to supplement store-purchased foods with self-provisioning.

In Fig. 10.2, we illustrate the extent of Indigenous landholdings in a Western legal sense, following land rights and native title reparation processes since the 1970s. This is a map that we have developed and updated on several occasions since 2015 (Altman & Markham, 2015). The totality of these holdings, sometimes referred to as "the Indigenous estate", covers more than half of remote and very remote Australia, comprising 4 million square kilometres. In terms of the supply chain heuristic examined in this book, the map highlights the proximity of discrete Indigenous communities and resident landowners to sources of *naturally* occurring foods rather than remoteness and transport challenges for accessing purchased food.

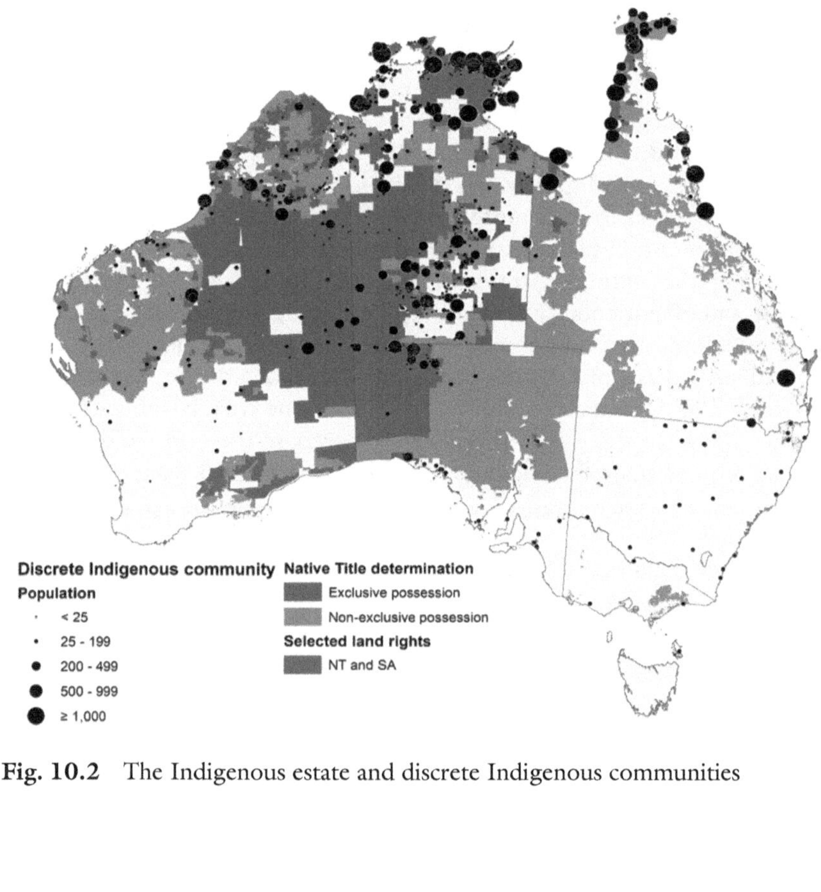

Fig. 10.2 The Indigenous estate and discrete Indigenous communities

What is especially significant is that native title law confers a set of rights and interests on Indigenous landowners that include the right to hunt, fish and forage on the land and waters; have access to and use of the natural waters of the land; and have a right to share or exchange subsistence and other traditional resources obtained on or from the land. While the law stipulates at section 211(2) of the *Native Title Act* 1993 (Cth) that such rights are limited to satisfying the personal, domestic or non-commercial communal needs of native-title holders, the distinction between commercial and non-commercial is an arbitrary colonial imposition that Indigenous people constantly challenge. To secure such rights and interests, a claimant must prove continuity of custom and tradition that is everywhere inclusive of animals, plants and other natural resources. This is an extraordinary resource right over a massive Indigenous jurisdiction. Hence, our use of the term "food sovereignty" is not speculative or conceptual. Rather, we recognize that Indigenous groups retain sovereign and legally recognized rights to lands and the food sources they provide on a continental scale.

COVID-19 policy shifts from April 2020 saw a punitive social-security approach suspended to facilitate social distancing. Although conducting research based on direct observation has been impossible because of lockdowns and the operation of biosecurity laws, there has been indirect evidence that both the Coronavirus Supplement and the suspension of mutual obligations have had positive impacts on self-provisioning for two main reasons.

First, as Markham and Altman (2019) have quantitatively demonstrated, the imposition of financial penalties for breaching mutual obligations reduced the incomes of the unemployed by an estimated 6 per cent. Such penalties further impoverished those already living below the poverty line. The suspension of mutual obligations and penalties would have conversely lifted people's incomes by this amount alongside the Coronavirus Supplement.

Second, as the unemployed were freed from mutual obligation requirements that required the able bodied to turn up for make-work and training daily for at least four hours under the Community Development Programme, they were able to visit, and in some cases, move back to, their customary lands to self-provision. Available qualitative research summarized by Staines et al. (2021, pp. 14–15) indicates that with additional income and available time, people were able to visit their Country and participate in hunting and gathering activities. Smith et al. (2020), working in the Northern Territory, report that "more people are going out camping and fishing … eating that bush tucker again … looking more healthy" and getting "away from the worries of town". In Arnhem Land, it was reported that people were returning to their Country to live in less crowded and healthier housing and source and eat bush foods (Altman, 2020).

In short, we argue that the perceived food security "crisis" in remote indigenous Australia is in large measure an artefact of pre-pandemic government policies that invariably impoverish the disproportionately high number of Indigenous unemployed. Such impoverishment can be offset in part by activating local and regional food supply chains. As the unemployed enjoyed more income and freedom in 2020, there was enhanced self-provisioning. Alongside enhanced purchase of food from stores, additional income allowed the purchase of essential equipment, including transport, needed today to exercise food sovereignty. Activating adjacent local and regional supply chains of naturally occurring foods can partly offset the high cost of purchased food at the end of long distribution supply chains.

Conclusion: Food and Coronavirus Supply Chains

Anna Tsing (2009) has theorized how the processes of supply chain capitalism create global standardization while generating growing gaps between rich and poor. Here, we have focused on disparities between Indigenous Australians and others, those living in the sparsely populated remote north and centre and those living in the more densely populated south. We show that those living at the very end of global food supply chains are subject to imposed technical solutions to the challenges posed by remoteness, while at the same time the historical and politico-structural circumstances that have created and maintained Indigenous poverty and marginalization are overlooked. The promise of economic salvation is predicated on paid work that does not exist, alongside an enduring myopia about actual livelihood possibilities where people live and can access land and its resources.

Emerging future-focused possibilities for self-provisioning are limited by government policy and escalating impoverishment. In remote Australia, surplus populations are located alongside growing availability of land and natural resources. People in such places have limited prospects for paid work. The social contract with the state sees income support delivered without any compensatory reference to local costs at the end of the global food supply chain. Indeed, the liberal settler state is highly ambiguous as to whether it seeks to make its policies "make live" or "let die" (Li, 2010). At the discursive and performative level, government policy looks to "make live" with cheaper, supposedly healthy store food, but actions to "make live" by increasing incomes or enhancing prospects for food sovereignty are not countenanced. The growing dependence on the store is becoming more and more embedded, while the scope to access legally guaranteed natural resources is rendered next to impossible.

We began our chapter with reference to a parliamentary inquiry urgently convened during the early days of the COVID-19 pandemic to examine issues of food pricing and food insecurity in remote Indigenous communities. Unsurprisingly, the inquiry reported that food prices for people living at the very end of global food supply chains are high, while poverty means that people experienced high levels of food insecurity. The inquiry recommended technical and regulatory actions to reduce prices at stores. Paradoxically, perhaps, the long and tenuous supply chains had a positive effect in assisting to keep remote Indigenous Australia relatively free of the coronavirus to date, with few infections and deaths in the first year of the pandemic. But the inquiry also opened a Pandora's box of questions about the many development challenges that remote Indigenous communities face daily. Food security cannot come from the store alone because people do not earn enough to pay for expensive food. So, we contend, either income-support payments need to increase or much more food needs to be derived from self-provisioning in the hinterland, beyond the store and the reach of the state.

References

Altman, J. (2020). *Submission No. 15 to the House of Representatives inquiry into food pricing and food security in remote indigenous communities.* Parliament of Australia, Canberra. Retrieved September 7, 2021, from https://www.aph.gov.au/Parliamentary_Business/Committees/House/Indigenous_Affairs/Foodpricing/Submissions

Altman, J., & Markham, F. (2015). Burgeoning indigenous land ownership: Diverse values and strategic potentialities. In S. Brennan, M. Davis, B. Edgeworth, & L. Terrill (Eds.), *Native title from Mabo to Akiba: A vehicle for change and empowerment?* (pp. 126–142). The Federation Press.

Arnhem Land Progress Aboriginal Corporation. (2020). *Annual report 2019–20.* Retrieved September 7, 2021, from https://www.alpa.asn.au/Handlers/Download.ashx?IDMF=6ba6ae4e-0c1b-487e-bdeb-82d80f63d07c

Australian Bureau of Statistics. (2019). *National Aboriginal and Torres Strait Islander Health Survey*. Retrieved September 7, 2021, from https://www.abs.gov.au/statistics/people/aboriginal-and-torres-strait-islander-peoples/national-aboriginal-and-torres-strait-islander-health-survey/latest-release

Buchanan, G. (2014). Hybrid economy research in remote indigenous Australia: Seeing and supporting the customary in community food economies. *Local Environment, 19*(1), 10–32.

Commonwealth of Australia. (2020). *Report on food pricing and food security in remote indigenous communities*. House of Representatives Standing Committee on Indigenous Affairs, Parliament of Australia. Retrieved September 7, 2021, from https://www.aph.gov.au/Parliamentary_Business/Committees/House/Indigenous_Affairs/Foodpricing/Report

Ferguson, M., Brown, C., Georga, C., Miles, E., & Brimblecombe, J. (2017). Traditional food availability and consumption in remote Aboriginal communities in the Northern Territory. *Australian and New Zealand Journal of Public Health, 41*(3), 294–298.

Fredericks, B., & Bradfield, A. (2021). Indigenous Australians and COVID-19: Highlighting ongoing food security issues. *International Journal of Home Economics, 14*(1), 53–65.

Keene, M. (2020). *COVID-19 and indigenous Australians: A chronology*. Parliamentary Library. Retrieved September 9, 2021, from https://parlinfo.aph.gov.au/parlInfo/download/library/prspub/7467598/upload_binary/7467598.pdf

Li, T. M. (2010). To make live or let die: Rural dispossession and the protection of surplus populations. *Antipode, 41*, 66–93.

Markham, F., & Altman, J. (2019). *Submission No. 77 to the Senate inquiry into the adequacy of Newstart and related payments*. Parliament of Australia, Canberra. Retrieved September 9, 2021, from https://www.aph.gov.au/Parliamentary_Business/Committees/Senate/Community_Affairs/Newstartrelatedpayments/Submissions accessed 7 September 2021

Markham, F., & Biddle, N. (2018). *Income, poverty and inequality*. CAEPR 2016 Census Paper No. 2. Canberra: The Australian National University. Retrieved September 9, 2021, from http://hdl.handle.net/1885/145053

Markham, F., & Kerins, S. (2020). Submission No. 30 to the inquiry into food pricing and food security in remote Indigenous communities. Retrieved September 7, 2021, from https://www.aph.gov.au/Parliamentary_Business/Committees/House/Indigenous_Affairs/Foodpricing/Submissions

Markham, F., Smith, D., & Morphy, F. (Eds.). (2020). *Indigenous Australians and the COVID-19 crisis: Perspectives on public policy. CAEPR Topical Issue 1/2020*. The Australian National University. Retrieved September 7, 2021, from https://openresearch-repository.anu.edu.au/bitstream/1885/202733/1/CAEPR_TI_no1_2020_Markham_Smith_Morphy.pdf

Martin, K., & Yanagisako, S. (2020). States of dependence: Introduction. *Social Anthropology, 28*(3), 646–656.

Outback Stores. (2020). *Annual report 2019–20.* Retrieved September 7, 2021, from https://outbackstores.com.au/wp-content/uploads/2020/12/OS-Annual-Report-20-web-spread.pdf

Smith, C., Kearney, A., Kotarba-Morely, A., Wilson, C., Grant, J., Pollard, K., & Saikia, U.. (2020). Friday essay: Voices from the bush—how lockdown affects remote Indigenous communities differently. *The Conversation*, May 15. 7 Retrieved September 7, 2021, from https://theconversation.com/friday-essay-voices-from-the-bush-how-lockdown-affects-remote-indigenous-communities-differently-136953

Staines, Z., Altman, J., Klein, E., & Markham, F. (2021). *Guiding principles for a new livelihood and work program in remote Indigenous Australia.* Discussion Paper. The Australia Institute. Retrieved September 7, 2021, from https://australiainstitute.org.au/wp-content/uploads/2021/08/P1124-Guiding-principles-for-a-new-livelihood-and-work-program-in-remote-Indigenous-Australia-Web.pdf

Tsing, A. (2009). Supply chains and the human condition. *Rethinking Marxism, 41*(2), 148–176.

CHAPTER 11

The UN Food Systems Summit: Disaster Capitalism and the Future of Food

Tomaso Ferrando

Abstract COVID-19 has brought to light the multiple cracks in the logistically integrated, financialized and commodity-based capitalist food system. As with other aspects of social life thrown into disruption amid the global health, economic and environmental downturn, the early weeks of the pandemic seemed to offer the hope of transformative possibility, a "portal" towards different food systems. The time seemed ripe for the kinds of radical transitions that social movements and peasants' organizations have requested for decades: subverting the "conventional" food system without going back to "corporate normality". However, when the multiple crises are characterized as exceptional rather than structural, a narrative of emergency and urgency is deployed to reinforce the power of the incumbents. The overlap between the pandemic and the climate crisis can be an opportunity, but hardly for peasants and indigenous people. As in Naomi Klein's *Shock Doctrine*, corporate actors and billionaire philanthropists are using the rhetoric of urgency to push for changes that reinforce the status quo and do not address the root causes that have brought

T. Ferrando (✉)
Faculty of Law (Law and Development Research Group), Institute of Development Policy (IOB), University of Antwerp, Antwerp, Belgium
e-mail: Tomaso.Ferrando@uantwerpen.be

V. Stead, M. Hinkson (eds.), *Beyond Global Food Supply Chains*,
https://doi.org/10.1007/978-981-19-3155-0_11

us here. In order to spark debate and reflections, my contribution engages with one example of ongoing co-optation of the state of climate and sanitary emergency: the 2021 United Nations Food Systems Summit as a new food policy arena where decisions are distanced from peasants, indigenous communities and citizens and put in the hands of corporations, financial investors and billionaire philanthropists.

Keywords Multi-stakeholderism • UN food systems summit • People's summit • Great reset • Food systems governance

Introduction

The COVID-19 pandemic has had an impact akin to that of a "natural" disaster on the global capitalist food system. It has magnified and intensified the socio-economic cracks that compose its texture, and it has devoured people and their relationships (Viner, 2020). Since the beginning of 2020 the world has experienced skyrocketing levels of food poverty: in 2020, the number of people going hungry was 15 per cent higher than in 2019. Food shortages have been experienced in the Global North and the Global South, and the overexposure of underpaid food workers to the risk of infection has been widely documented (e.g. see Bogoeski, 2021). Worldwide, farmers and consumers dependent on international trade, along with informal and local food traders, have been hit by the temporary paralysis of the global logistic infrastructure. Producers have suffered as a result of reductions in global demand for particular products, the closure of informal and local markets, and the implementation of more rigid health and safety restrictions.

At the same time, climate change and the loss of social and biological diversity are ravaging the planet. The year 2020 registered the increasing probability of record-shattering climate extremes (Fischer et al., 2021), and it was one of the three warmest years on record, with a global average temperature of 1.2 degrees Celsius above pre-industrial (1850–1900) levels. There was heavy rain and extensive flooding over large parts of Africa and Asia. There were wildfires, droughts and 30 named storms in the North Atlantic hurricane season—the largest number of named storms on record (World Meteorological Organization, 2020). According to the International Federation of Red Cross and Red Crescent Societies (IFRC, 2020), more than 50 million people were doubly hit in 2020 by climate-related disasters and by the pandemic, a situation that worsened food insecurity and added another layer of risk to disaster-related evacuation, recovery and relief operations.

Just a few months into the pandemic, it was clear to many that the global food system was incapable of providing adequate daily nutrition for the world's population, let alone delivering a good life for those who participate in food production or a promising future for the environment and the planet. The intensity and transnational nature of the shocks felt on the ground were such that the time seemed ripe for the radical transformation that indigenous people, grassroots organizations and peasants' organizations have been pursuing for decades. Suddenly, the need to address hunger, food security and the link between food systems, climate change and the loss of biological and social diversity were placed prominently on political agendas. From individual villages and cities to the United Nations, voices were raised in passionate advocacy of the need to rethink the future of the food system, the future for workers and the future of the planet. For many, the slogan "we shall not go back to normality because normality was the problem" that was projected on a building in Santiago de Chile during the first weeks of lockdown was equally applicable to the economic and food systems.

Might we suggest that the COVID-19 pandemic is the straw that broke the capitalist food system's back? Without any presumption of completeness, this chapter explores a recent set of events that reveal ongoing attempts by corporate actors, governments, academics and billionaire philanthropists to co-opt the climate change and health "emergency" in conjunction with the rhetoric of an "urgent need for change" in food systems. While they agree on the need to rapidly transform the food system, their goal is to implement paradigms, visions and "solutions" that reinforce the inequality and structural misery entrenched in capitalist food systems. This is the United Nations Food Systems Summit that took place on 23 September 2021 and that was anticipated over summer 2021 by the Science Days and the pre-summit. The summit represents an attempt by the global political and economic elite to highjack the dynamics of global food governance. The UN Committee on World Food Security and the High Level Panel of Experts reject bottom-up and radical solutions and rather promote a "multi-stakeholder" approach to food that deploys technological and digital innovations. In this approach, critical decisions about the future of food are depoliticized, distanced from peasants, indigenous communities and citizens and aligned with the interests of the status quo and their modernist and techno-optimist approach to systemic socio-environmental challenges.

The political and intellectual "violence" of the summit has not gone unnoticed. In the last months, it has been a catalyst for a multiplicity of social movements, indigenous groups, food workers, academics and others who oppose the domination of food systems by the state and capital interests (Van Apeldoorn et al., 2012). As the dispute unfolds, this chapter unpacks the circumstances under which the counter-movement is unfolding. It argues for the need to focus on the legacy of the summit and its promotion of a hegemonic vision that is pushed through the rhetorical and procedural mechanisms of disaster capitalism (Polanyi, 1944).

Multiple Pandemic Disruptions: An Opportunity for Whom?

Since the first months of lockdown in early 2020, a series of high-profile writers have offered critical commentaries on the relationship between the present and future subversion of people and the planet. While not specifically addressing the future of food, those commentaries are relevant here. In April 2020, for example, Arundhati Roi (2020) wrote that the pandemic offered "us a chance to rethink the doomsday machine we have built for ourselves. Nothing could be worse than a return to normality". For Roy, the virus that "made the mighty kneel" could have opened a "portal", a "gateway between one world and the next". For Naomi Klein, like a great depression or a war, the pandemic and the extension of the public financial interventions in the Global North possessed the radicalizing potential for big and positive changes; however, they would have to be fought for (Viner, 2020). For Achille Mbembe, on the contrary, the intensification of the state of emergency due to the spread of the pandemic had strengthened the logic of sacrifice that "has always been at the centre of neo-liberalism, which has always worked with the idea that someone is worth more than others" (García, 2020). Rather than an opportunity for emancipation, Mbembe suggests, recent events have seen the normalization of the most violent tendencies of contemporary society.

Each of these analyses could be deployed to describe processes unfolding in the context of food systems, in the North as well as the South. Globally, peasants, activists and their allies have been engaging in acts of solidarity. They have joined hands to provide protection against COVID-19 and carried out exchanges among peasants on the production of healthy food and "donated food, seed, produced and distributed hygiene and protective materials" (La Via Campesina, 2020) in countries where they are based, such as Zambia, Zimbabwe, Venezuela, Haiti and Palestine. In several cities in the North, people organized food-solidarity activities to fill the gaps of the existing "short-term, scattered, top-down and underfunded initiatives [that] have been both the cause and the consequence of the current food poverty crisis" (Lombardozzi et al., 2021). People gathered momentum to promote local strategies of solidarity, often in contraposition with both market and state. At the same time, however, already in August 2020 La Via Campesina reported that governments had detained, beaten and harassed volunteers at community-led soup kitchens, implemented strict checkpoints that discouraged peasants from reaching their farmlands, collaborated with private actors to forcefully evict villagers, and reformed labour, land and other forms of legal protection in order to facilitate the flow of foreign investments and a quick economic recovery (La Via Campesina, 2020; Ferrando & Vecchione Gonçalves, 2020).

The struggles that are taking place on the ground are reproduced internationally and globally. Yet at a distance from the localism of solidarity and collaboration, the urgent need to transform food systems has been progressively co-opted within the dominant capitalist framework and has triggered political processes whose outcomes will run significantly at odds with the needs and rights of the billions of smallholders who produce most of the world's food as well as the ecological needs of the web of life (Capra, 1997). This process of co-optation does not unfold evenly or homogenously. Often, co-optation occurs by replacing the political concepts promoted "from below" with "sterile" and technical ideas that sidestep issues of power, ecological justice and rights. In other cases, it happens through the strategic use of fear and imminence to legitimize policy changes that are blind to the socio-environmental complexity of food systems and serve to reproduce the capitalist mode of production. Even when narratives identify human rights and agroecology, these concepts are treated as addenda or "extra" or refigured as ideas about "nature positive food systems" and "carbon neutrality" that push the future of food away from the aspirations of peasants, indigenous communities and citizens and into the hands of corporations, financial investors and billionaire philanthropists.

The pandemic has seen the intensification of the global capitalist food system, amplifying existing critical social and environmental conditions and making more urgent the need for transformative intervention. In the same period multiple bottom-up and grassroots initiatives have been calling out the shortcomings of a system that treats food as a commodity rather than a public good, a right and a commons (Vivero Pol et al., 2018). However, the shocks to the food systems are not only opening new possibilities for radical transformation but also creating the rhetorical and material conditions for the intensification of processes of marginalization, commodification, dispossession and appropriation (Harvey, 2003). Echoing Naomi Klein's (2007) analysis of the aftermath of Hurricane Katrina in New Orleans, instrumental narratives of "urgency" have been deployed to frame pandemic disruptions of the food system, consolidating the power of political, financial and food elites to the detriment of peasants, indigenous people and non-commodified food systems (Agamben, 1998, 2008). Global food governance appears to be experiencing an intensification of "disaster capitalism" wherein national and transnational governmental institutions instrumentalize the catastrophe "to promote and empower a range of private, neoliberal capitalist interests" (Schuller & Maldonado, 2016, p. 62). At the international and European level, the fight for the future of food has never been so intense.

Food Systems Summit to Put Corporate Priorities on the Menu

On 16 October 2019, World Food Day, the United Nations Secretary-General, António Guterres, announced to the Plenary of the UN Committee on World Food Security that he would organize a high-level UN Food Systems Summit as part of the Decade of Action to deliver the Sustainable Development Goals. The summit had been jointly requested by the UN Food and Agricultural Organization, the International Fund for Agricultural Development, the World Food Programme and the World Economic Forum. Originally planned for autumn 2020, the summit was postponed to September 2021 as a result of the pandemic (One Planet Network, 2019). At the time of writing, a few weeks before the summit and few weeks after the July pre-summit in Rome, the processes, forms of participation, power dynamics and goals of the summit remain unclear and contested.

Since Guterres' announcement, several things have changed in the world and in the narrative around the Food Systems Summit. A gathering that was originally aimed at creating a world free of hunger by:

> affirming the centrality of food systems to the achievement of the 2030 Agenda, aligning stakeholders involved in food systems transformation around a common practical framework, strengthening evidence and developing tools for decision makers to make choices on trade-offs, promoting a science-policy interface on food systems, and accelerating multi-stakeholder actions at different levels. (One Planet Network, 2019)

is now presented as the last call to deal with the "urgency" of reshaping "food systems so they support healthy diets for all and do more to make food production and consumption aligned to sustainable development" (United Nations, 2020, p. 2). For the United Nations (2020, p. 4): "This crisis can serve as a turning point to rebalance and transform our food systems, making them more inclusive, sustainable and resilient".

Although there is generalized agreement about the need to address the social and environmental injustices that stem from and affect the global food system, the question is whether the Food Systems Summit is the appropriate space and its invitees the right people to recognize that the "sickness" of the system is not a peripheral issue but a central issue of their own making (Mozo, 2013). To paraphrase Susan Marks (2011), it is important to question whether the sense of "urgency" and "emergency" will lead to comprehensive reflection on the state of misery entrenched in food systems and a commitment to interrogate root causes or whether structural incoherence and tensions will be overshadowed by calls for more technology, more manipulation of nature and the application of bandages to a "capitalist ecosystem" that is chronically ill.

The risk of co-optation of the disruptive effects of COVID-19 and the related state of emergency have not gone unnoticed. Since Guterres' announcement, the summit has been challenged by civil society organizations and indigenous people who are part of the Civil Society and Indigenous Peoples' Mechanism for relations with the UN Committee on World Food Security. For them and their allies, the summit and its rhetoric represent a direct attack on the Committee on World Food Security and the High Level Panel of Experts on Food Security and Nutrition as legitimate spaces that are accessible to the people who make food possible and that reflect the political nature of the global governance of food. Moreover, the summit has been presented as an attempt to highjack the "emergency" to promote an idea of "multi-stakeholderism" that puts foxes and chickens in the same coop (McKeon, 2017) and overlooks the structural incompatibilities between different visions of food systems. This rhetoric around the summit nurtures the false impression that "there is space for everyone around the table" while implementing an agenda based on a monolithic and Eurocentric understanding of progress, science and techno-fixes.

The co-optation is evident in the way the summit has been conceived, the boundaries of "expertise" defined and related knowledge produced. In mid-2019, a concept note circulated at the High-Level Political Forum indicated that the World Economic Forum would be involved in organizing the summit. Subsequently, the president of the Alliance for a Green Revolution in Africa was appointed by Guterres as the special envoy to the summit. The fact that the Alliance for a Green Revolution in Africa is a leader in the promotion of a "modernist" and "productivist" conception of the future of agriculture, based on genetically enhanced seeds, patents, close interaction with corporate actors and digitalization, immediately revealed the close connection between the summit and those interests. Similarly, corporate-sponsored organizations are present across the five "Action Tracks" that have had carriage of brainstorming and defining the future of the system. Moreover, a Scientific Group was established under the coordination of Professor Joachim Von Braun that organized a two-day event in early July 2021 and reinforced "recognition of the pivotal role of science, technology and innovation for food systems transformation" and aimed to "offer an important opportunity to support the agenda setting process with scientific evidence and perspectives" (United Nations, 2021).

These political and power dynamics led more than 400 indigenous, peasant and civil society organizations to write to UN Secretary-General Guterres in March 2020, challenging the summit as a space that does not draw "from the innovative governance experiences that the UN system has to offer, [but] is helping to establish stakeholder capitalism as a governance model for the entire planet" (Letter to H.E. Mr António Guterres, 2020). In their statement, the food activists requested that the partnership between the World Economic Forum and the Alliance for a Green Revolution in Africa be discontinued if the summit process was not to be derailed. In the absence of a satisfactory response, in February 2021, the Civil Society and Indigenous Peoples' Mechanism reached out to Guterres and announced that it would have not "jumped on a train going in the wrong direction" and, in the absence of substantial change in the structure, governance and purpose of the summit, would not participate.

Facing these criticisms, the Food Systems Summit bunkered down behind its own narrative of "inclusiveness" rather than recognize the tensions and incompatibility between visions. In line with the idea of a "Great Reset" promoted by Klaus Schwab (2021), the founder and executive chairman of the World Economic Forum and special envoy to the summit, Dr Agnes Kalibata, responded to the criticisms of co-optation by stressing the open nature of the summit and that everyone had a seat at the table. She strengthened the call for "multi-stakeholderism" and the idea of a "new social contract" as tools to overcome the ongoing impasse. According to Kalibata, what was required was the quick implementation of solutions that would increase the productivity, availability and sustainability of food systems.

In early March 2021, Kalibata published an article in *The Guardian* (on a page sponsored by the Bill and Melinda Gates Foundation, one of the sponsors of the Alliance for a Green Revolution in Africa) where she claimed:

> The entire purpose of the summit is to embrace not only the shared interests of all stakeholders but also—importantly—the areas of divergence on how we go about addressing the harsh reality humanity faces. If we are to build more inclusive food systems, we must be prepared to have inclusive debate. (Kalibata, 2021)

If everyone can speak, the social contract argument goes, the solution will inevitably be the one to benefit everyone—a compromise that takes everyone's perspective into account and leverages common aspirations and needs. If everyone puts aside their preconceptions and walks together in the same direction, we can reach the goal that everyone desires.

However, critical race approaches to liberalism and egalitarianism (Delgado & Stefancic, 1993, p. 462; Crenshaw, 1989, 1991), critical feminist accounts that read social contracts foregrounding inclusion as reproducing dualism and domination (Pateman, 1988), and recent accounts of the push towards "multi-stakeholderism" in food systems as an attempt to neutralize power dynamics (McKeon, 2017) teach us that such power-neutral visions of society lead to the misrecognition of existing inequalities, the consolidation of incumbent power structures, and the creation of new forms of exclusion and subordination. In the specific case of food systems, the idea that "coexistence" between capitalist and non-capitalist visions of food is possible is equally characterized by misrecognition of the expansionist and transformative impact of capitalism as a specific way of organizing people and nature. Genetically modified BT aubergines are promoted at the same time as agroecology. Gene editing and the restoration of the commons are discussed in the same context. Corporate power and its responsibility for the state of food systems are never discussed (Von Braun et al., 2021). In the context of radical power imbalances and competition over resources, what power has the subaltern to define the terms of this "coexistence"?

The need to address the role of corporations and corporate philanthropists in (not-so-silently) shaping the structure, agenda and future of food systems has become even more urgent in the events leading up to the summit. During the inauguration of the pre-summit, the chair of Imagine was invited to speak after heads of state, the European Commission and the World Bank. Imagine, the chair said, is an organization that helps businesses "eradicate poverty and inequality and stem runaway climate change" (the organization's website says Imagine helps "C-suites see their business' true place in the world" (Imagine, 2021)). He deployed the rhetoric that technology for change is available, that transforming food systems has the highest return from ecological, social and financial perspectives and that with relatively small investments ($300–400 billion) "we" can transform the food system into a positive economic force, doubling agricultural productivity with half the inputs currently used.

On the second day, a session on "Private Sector Priorities at the UN Food Systems Pre-Summit" included the president of the World Business Council for Sustainable Development and representatives of some of the largest food companies in the world (Nestlé, Unilever, PepsiCo). The session praised the publication of the Business Declaration for Food Systems Transformation as a vision that reinforces the role of corporate capital and its centrality in addressing social and environmental problems (as if these problems had been created by unknown forces or "natural" events). Discussion in this session summoned all the sustainability buzzwords to call for the urgent establishment of a food system that was "equitable, net zero, nature positive, resilient and capable of feeding all people". Planetary boundaries, soil healthiness, living income for all, regenerative agriculture and other key terms that would usually be leveraged in critiques of the capitalist food system have now been integrated into corporate speeches. Citing "urgency" and "stakeholderism", they shift attention away from questions of who is responsible for the ongoing misery of so many of the world's population (Marks, 2011) and stress the transformative role of large-scale corporate players.

For the president of Unilever's Foods & Refreshment division, for example, living income for all producers in their chain is a goal. However, corporations cannot achieve this on their own, a statement that clashes with Unilever's US$6.3 billion net income in 2020 and the steady distribution of dividends to shareholders that has been guaranteed in the last years. Thus, the future is that of a corporate-led global food system where farmers who capture carbon in the soil, "smart agricultural practices to achieve net-zero and nature positive food systems", digital technologies, innovations, collaboration among corporations around sustainability to maintain the same levels of financial return (Lombardi & Ferrando, 2021), and the adoption of policies and subsidies that support regenerative and nutritious agricultural practices, healthier consumption and reduced food loss and waste. Rather than the problem, corporations and their global power are presented as the solution. In the words of Nestlé's CEO: "the private sector is the implementation machine". For PepsiCo's chairperson: corporations have the "unique power of talking to a billion-plus consumers and have to educate them" to buy commodities that are better for the planet and the workers (Kuljay et al., 2021).

At this time of multiple structural social and ecological crises, the Food Systems Summit and its prequels (such as the Sciences Day and the pre-summit) represent more than a falsely inclusive process that promotes partnerships among unequals (Canfield et al., 2021). They resemble a classic capitalist attempt to co-opt and internalize critiques (such as poor working conditions, undernourishment and obesity) and terminology (like "planetary boundaries" and regenerative agriculture) to promote a mix of old and new technological and digital solutions that reinforce the idea that humans can control nature and shape societies, distract from the political nature of the struggle, overlook questions of who benefits, and entrench the reproduction of global capitalism. In this context, members of the Civil Society and Indigenous Peoples' Mechanism for relations with the UN Committee on World Food Security, academics and other civil society organizations refuse to legitimize this "new food space" and instead are organizing an alternative people's pre-summit and summit to debunk the procedure, narrative and outputs of the Food Systems Summit. However, resisting co-optation may not be enough. The new convergence of interests of private and public elites could represent an ominous further turning point in respect of the future of food and the web of life that makes it possible (Capra, 1997).

Conclusion

For billions of people around the world, COVID-19 and the climate emergency have shown that the capitalist and financialized food system is in a state of permanent emergency, a condition of intrinsic sickness that is inherent to its construction (Mozo, 2013). From the Global North to the Global South, the several months of compound disruptions have multiplied the reasons to think that the capitalist and financialized food system is not essential to the future of food but rather responsible for the social and environmental injustices that characterize its past and present. Who is essential to the future of the food systems? It is the billions of peasants and workers (mainly migrants) that farm, transform, transport, distribute and cook. It is the gift of nature and the regenerative capacity of soil and ecosystems to reproduce themselves (when they are not depleted). It is the predisposition of public policies that treat food as a public good (if not a commons), leverage responsibilities for social and environmental harms, redress historical inequalities and contribute to the establishment of democratic spaces of decision-making and governance.

The mainstream responses to the pandemic have contributed to the promotion of a particular rhetoric in relation to the present and future of food: the idea that urgency and misery are not structural and planned (Marks, 2011) but contingent upon and defined by an unfortunate combination of multiple factors that have little to do with capitalism and the idea that food is nothing but a commodity (United Nations, 2020). In this context, not only are the root causes of the problems overlooked but also the rhetoric and processes of the state of emergency are deployed to reinforce the status quo and promote solutions that do not challenge existing structures of power and accumulation. The United Nations Food Systems Summit, a "multi-stakeholder" event for digital and technological innovation, demonstrates this process in action.

At the same time, the political and economic violence of the summit has had a mobilizing effect on social movements, indigenous groups, food workers, human rights lawyers and academics and served to strengthen the interactions between those who oppose the domination of the food systems and their future shaping by contemporary configurations of state and capital (Van Apeldoorn et al., 2012). For them, the Food Systems Summit risks being the last nail in the coffin of food sovereignty, food democracy and food justice—a way of co-opting the moment of crisis while ignoring structural concerns around the circulation of power, inequality and profit.

These groups expose the deployment of "urgency" and "emergency" to transform those who are responsible for misery into saviours, the use of quick fixes in place of long-lasting solutions and the marginalization of pivotal concepts such as the right to food and self-determination. As the dispute unfolds before our eyes, we need to be attentive and critically engaged. Will the summit prove Mbembe right and consolidate the idea that someone (financialized capital) is worth more than others? Or will the counter-movement (Polanyi, 1944) be capable of defying the hegemonic vision promoted by the summit and succeed in destabilizing the mechanisms of disaster capitalism? What is clear is that disruptions in the time of COVID-19 have intensified processes and dynamics that have been unfolding for decades. Whatever radical potential exists will have to be fought for.

References

Agamben, G. (1998). *Homo Sacer: Sovereign power and bare life*. Stanford University Press.

Agamben, G. (2008). *State of exception*. University of Chicago Press.

Bogoeski, V. (2021, February 4). Beyond protection: Towards democratizing work in the meat industry. *WSI*. Retrieved August 16, 2021, from https://www.wsi.de/en/30352.htm

Canfield, M., Anderson, M. D., & McMichael, P. (2021, April 13). UN Food Systems Summit 2021: Dismantling democracy and resetting corporate control of food systems. *Frontiers in Sustainable Food Systems*. https://doi.org/10.3389/fsufs.2021.661552; https://www.frontiersin.org/articles/10.3389/fsufs.2021.661552/full

Capra, F. (1997). *The web of life*. Harper Collins.

Crenshaw, K. (1989). Demarginalizing the intersection of race and sex: A Black feminist critique of antidiscrimination doctrine, feminist theory and antiracist politic. *University of Chicago Legal Forum, 1*(8), 139–167.

Crenshaw, K. (1991). Mapping the margins: Intersectionality, identity politics, and violence against women of color. *Stanford Law Review, 43*(6), 1241–1299.

Delgado, R., & Stefancic, J. (1993). Critical race theory: An annotated bibliography. *Virginia Law Review, 79*(2), 461–516.

Ferrando, T., & Vecchione Gonçalves, M. (2020). Privatization and dispossession in the shadow of the pandemic. *Land Portal*. Retrieved July 30, 2021, from https://www.landportal.org/blog-post/2021/02/privatization-and-dispossession-shadow-pandemic

Fischer, E. M., Sippel, S., & Knutti, R. (2021). Increasing probability of record-shattering climate extremes. *Nature Climate Change, 11*, 689–695.

García, B. (2020, April 8). Post COVID-19: Will we be the same after the pandemic? *Al Día*. https://aldianews.com/articles/culture/social/post-covid-19-will-we-be-same-after-pandemic/58120
Harvey, D. (2003). *The new imperialism*. Oxford University Press.
IFRC. (2020, November 17). *World disasters report 2020. Come heat or high water: tackling the humanitarian impacts of the climate crisis together*. Reliefweb. Accessed July 30 2021, from https://reliefweb.int/report/world/world-disasters-report-2020-come-heat-or-high-water-tackling-humanitarian-impacts
Imagine. (2021). Accessed September 15, 2021, from https://imagine.one/
Kalibata, A. (2021, March 9). The UN food systems summit will consider all stakeholders' interests, *The Guardian*. https://www.theguardian.com/global-development/2021/mar/09/the-un-food-systems-summit-will-consider-all-stakeholders-interests
Klein, N. (2007). *The shock doctrine: The rise of disaster capitalism*. Metropolitan Books.
Kuljay, A., Louvin, J. M., Anderson, M., Jaffer, N., & Ferrando, T. (2021, September 12). From food as a commodity to food as liberation. *Development*.
La Via Campesina. (2020). The winds of change are blowing harder: COVID-19 update on peasants, rural workers and other marginalized groups. *La Via Campesina*. Retrieved July 30, 2021, from https://viacampesina.org/en/the-winds-of-change-are-blowing-harder-covid-19-update-on-peasants-rural-workers-and-other-marginalized-groups/
Letter to H.E. Mr António Guterres, UN Secretary-General. (2020). Accessed September 15, 2021. https://www.foodsovereignty.org/wp-content/uploads/2020/03/EN_Edited_draft-letter-UN-food-systems-summit_070220.pdf
Lombardi, C., & Ferrando, T. (2021). An environmentally and socially broken global food system: What role for competition law? In S. Holmes et al. (Eds.), *Competition law, climate change and environmental sustainability* (pp. 339–349). Concurrences.
Lombardozzi, L., Copperman, J., & Auma, C. I. (2021). *Food poverty and urban struggles during COVID-19: The social reproduction of unequal London and the false narrative about the "pandemic-led crisis"*. IKD Working Paper No. 89. Milton Keynes: The Open University.
Marks, S. (2011). Human rights and root causes. *Modern Law Review, 74*(1), 57–78.
McKeon, N. (2017). Are equity and sustainability a likely outcome when foxes and chickens share the same coop? Critiquing the concept of multistakeholder governance of food security. *Globalizations, 14*(3), 379–398.
Mozo, C. (2013). Aportaciones y Potencialidades de la Antropología de la Salud. *Revista Andaluza de Antropología, 5*, 1–11.
One Planet Network. (2019, November 1). UN Food Systems Summit announced. *One Planet Network*. Retrieved August 16, 2021, from https://www.oneplanetnetwork.org/UN-food-systems-summit-announcement
Pateman, C. (1988). *The sexual contract*. Stanford University Press.

Pol, V., Luis, J., Ferrando, T., Mattei, U., & De Schutter, O. (2018). *Routledge handbook of food as a commons*. Routledge.
Polanyi, K. (1944). *The great transformation*. Farrar & Rinehart.
Roi, A. (2020, April 3). The pandemic is a portal. *The Financial Times*.
Schuller, M., & Maldonado, J. (2016). Disaster capitalism. *Annals of Anthropological Practice, 40*(1), 61–72.
Schwab, K. (2021). *Stakeholder capitalism: A global economy that works for progress, people and planet*. John Wiley & Sons.
United Nations. (2020). *Policy brief: The impact of COVID-19 on food security and nutrition*. United Nations.
United Nations. (2021). Food systems summit, Scientific Group, About Us. United Nations. https://sc-fss2021.org/
Van Apeldoorn, B., de Graaff, N., & Overbeek, H. (2012). The reconfiguration of the global state-capital nexus. *Globalizations, 9*(4), 471–486.
Viner, K. (2020, July 13). Naomi Klein: We must not return to the pre-Covid status quo, only worse. *The Guardian*.
Von Braun, J., Afsana, K., Fresco, L., & Hassan, M. (2021, September 2). Food systems: Seven priorities to end hunger and protect the planet. *Nature, 597*, 28–30.
World Meteorological Organization. (2020). *State of the global climate 2020*. World Meteorological Organization. Retrieved July 30, 2021, from https://public.wmo.int/en/media/press-release/climate-change-indicators-and-impacts-worsened-2020

CHAPTER 12

Against Consumer Ethics

Christopher Mayes and Angie Sassano

Abstract Consumer food ethics has re-emerged over the past 30 years as a popular form of activism to address concerns with the dominance of corporate interests in the global food system. Proponents of consumer ethics contend that informing consumers about injustices in the food system via labels or awareness campaigns will lead to collective rejection of unethical food corporations and the embrace of ethical products. This approach has been criticized on a variety of grounds, including its reliance on and eventual co-optation by market mechanisms. In response to these criticisms, food activists and scholars have promoted a consumer ethic that embraces local and alternative food systems, thereby producing an alternative consumer ethic purportedly outside of market logics. While these alternative practices have much to commend them, we argue that alternative food systems are invariably oriented towards consumer interests and thereby run into similar problems faced by earlier iterations of consumer-based ethics. We argue against the persistent focus on consumer ethics as means of substantially disrupting food systems, whether global, local or alternative.

Keywords Consumer ethics • Ethical consumption • Alternative food

---

C. Mayes (✉) • A. Sassano
Alfred Deakin Institute, Deakin University, Waurn Ponds, VIC, Australia
e-mail: christopher.mayes@deakin.edu.au; asassano@deakin.edu.au

V. Stead, M. Hinkson (eds.), *Beyond Global Food Supply Chains*,
https://doi.org/10.1007/978-981-19-3155-0_12

Introduction

The global and industrialized food system has enabled the production and distribution of cheaper, longer-lasting and more diverse food items. We can enjoy tropical fruits in winter, purchase whole chickens for the same price as a cup of coffee and eat fresh bread long after it has been baked. Once celebrated as the benevolent results of food science, the ingenuity of farmers and sophisticated global logistics, these cheap foods are increasingly dismissed as the tainted fruits of Big Food—the culinary version of Big Pharma, Big Tobacco and Big Oil.

Activists and scholars have pointed to unethical practices in global food production since at least the sugar boycotts of the eighteenth century. Over the past 30 years, food activists and scholars have renewed efforts to draw attention to the negative effects of the global food system on the environment, farm workers, animal welfare and human health. Documentary films and books on the exploits of Big Food have become a profitable sub-genre of the entertainment industry and propelled the issues and their authors to the spotlight. Books by Michael Pollan, Eric Schlosser and Marion Nestle, as well as associated feature films such as *Fast Food Nation* (2006), *Food, Inc.* (2008), *Farmageddon* (2011), *Fed Up* (2014) and *Seaspiracy* (2021), have popularized concerns about the negative effects of the global food system. In addition, awareness campaigns and labelling schemes attempt to bring the ethical and political realities of food to consumer attention at the purchase point. Ethical labelling such as "Fair Trade" characterizes food choice as a matter not simply of taste or convenience but of ethical and political importance.

Underlying these campaigns, labels and films is the shared belief that consumers have been kept ignorant of the truth by multinational food corporations and neoliberal governments; if consumers are enlightened, they will use their collective purchasing power to transform, or at least alter, industry activities. The basic idea is that by knowing what is in our food and how it was cultivated, harvested, produced and distributed, we will reject unethical food corporations and buy from ethical producers, thereby disrupting unjust practices. Belief in the power of truth to awaken the slumbering consumer giant was evoked in mid-1990s anti-global capital movements. In the introduction to her landmark book, *No Logo* (2002), Naomi Klein outlines her hypothesis: "as more people discover the brand-name secrets of the global logo web, their outrage will fuel the next big political movement, a vast wave of opposition squarely targeting transnational corporations, particularly those with very high name-brand recognition" (Klein, 2002). According to Klein, when the veil is removed and people discover the "secrets" behind their consumer products, an outrage—or at least changed consumer behaviours—will be unleashed, transforming the global web of capital. This logic is echoed in calls for food labels to reveal the unethical production practices of Big Food (Wells, 2016).

There is a diverse literature revealing the limits of ethico-political consumption (Carrington et al., 2021). In this chapter, we briefly explore three: the transformation of citizens into consumers; the co-optation of consumer ethics by the market; and the dominance of consumer interests in determining what is ethically salient. We conclude by examining whether calls for alternative food systems can offer a disruption to the global food system or whether it is at risk of consumer co-optation.

Consumers Not Citizens

An initial criticism of ethical consumption is that citizens are transformed into consumers, reducing political action to consumption (Soper & Trentmann, 2008). Holding governments and companies accountable for unethical practices therefore becomes a matter of consumer choice rather than systemic change. Basing ethical and political action in consumer practices is a problem for at least two reasons. First, this approach is regressive in that it places a greater burden on the financially less well off to act ethically. Second, it is a thin and privatized approach to ethico-political action, ultimately serving to absolve one's individual guilt while allowing injustices to continue.

The claim that this approach is regressive is quite straightforward. As Thomas Wells (2016) outlines in his argument for labels exposing animal cruelty, they would allow better but more expensive standards of animal welfare. This phenomenon is repeatedly seen in the market, where products purporting to be more ethical, just or environmentally sustainable are considerably more expensive than the standard product as they include the "real" costs of production. As such, to enact one's ethical and political preferences requires a sufficient income, thereby making ethico-political consumption more achievable for the wealthy and less so for those on lower incomes. This scenario leaves some individuals feeling incapable of enacting their moral and political beliefs due to financial constraints, while others feel that they have fully discharged theirs. This criticism has been made by several scholars across a variety of disciplines (Carrington et al., 2021, p. 227).

The second claim, that consumption is a thin and privatized approach to ethical action, is less straightforward. The political thought of Hannah Arendt is useful for articulating the distinction between consumer and citizen (Arendt, 1998). For Arendt, citizens actively participate in collective deliberation about the values of the political community or *polis*. Citizens have duties, obligations and rights and are situated within a public political community recognized by political institutions. While citizenship is a problematic category in its exclusivity, and we do not wish to imply that meaningful political action is only performed within the parameters of citizenship, the consumer, by contrast, has a substantially narrowed set of duties, obligations and rights, often defined by private individual preferences (Arendt, 1977). For Arendt, the satisfaction of individual preferences is secondary to politics, and if it becomes primary, it has a corrosive effect on the public sphere and political action. Rather than participating in and helping shape a *polis*, the consumer is in the market seeking to fulfil their private interests. Therefore, focusing on the consumer restricts ethical and political action to the supermarket aisles and home pantry. While ethics as a consumer preference may be acceptable in some disputable cases—for instance, whether one chooses to eat animal products—in other cases, such as those involving slavery or contributing to ecological collapse, the ethical dilemma reaches beyond private consumer preference. Choices permitting slavery or practices that jeopardize the ecological integrity required for sustaining life rest on prior political questions about the nature and character of the political community and the possibility of its continuance. Consequently, these choices cannot be left to private consumer choice but require public political deliberation and action (Arendt, 1998, p. 7).

Consumer Co-optation

A second problem with ethico-political consumption is that the consumer response is susceptible to co-optation by the very corporations that are being protested against. Due to the vast array of products sold by transnational corporations, it is possible for corporations to maintain highly profitable but "unethical" products along with less profitable but "ethical" ones. For example, Pace Farm is one of the largest producers of cage eggs in Australia, yet it sells free-range eggs, too. It also owns other brands, such as Family Value, that are not obviously associated with Pace Farm.

The poverty of this situation can be more fully understood through Ivan Illich's concept of "radical monopoly". A monopoly is generally understood as one corporation having control over a market. Illich (1973) uses the example of Coca-Cola's monopoly over the soft-drink market in Nicaragua: if a Nicaraguan wants a cold drink, their only options are Coke or water. These sorts of monopolies "restrict the choices open to the consumer" (Illich, 1973, p. 57). A radical monopoly, however, according to Illich, means "the dominance of the one type of product rather than the dominance of one brand" (Illich, 1973, p. 57). To use Illich's example, in large cities such as Los Angeles, cars monopolize traffic and shape urban infrastructure such that other forms of transport are eliminated. It is that the dominance of the car "curtails the right to walk, not that more people drive Chevies than Fords, [that] constitutes radical monopoly" (Illich, 1973, p. 57).

In a similar way, large supermarkets exert a radical monopoly over distribution of and access to food. For example, it is almost impossible for the majority of Australians to avoid the supermarket. As such, consumer choice, ethical or otherwise, occurs within the context of a for-profit distribution system that effectively eliminates other possibilities of engaging with the harvesting, production and distribution of food. The potency of ethico-political consumption—the proverbial "voting with your wallet"—is captured by the very forces that actors are trying to resist. Even if ethical labels and awareness campaigns serve to disrupt corporate brands, they also trap individuals into responsibility for systemic and global issues, such as public health, global poverty, animal welfare or fair working conditions. This is not to say that the consumer is absolved but that the idea that more consumption will solve the problems of consumption is self-defeating.

Consumer Self-Interest

A third criticism is the way consumer interests dominate and set the terms of what is ethically salient. In 1905 Upton Sinclair wrote *The Jungle* to highlight the hazardous working conditions of Chicago's meatpacking industry. His US audience, however, was more horrified by the sanitary conditions, which resulted in the *Pure Food and Drug Act* 1906. This improved food sanitation for consumers but neglected the conditions for the workers (Kantor, 1976), which led Sinclair to quip, "I aimed for the public's heart, and by accident hit it in the stomach". Likewise today, much of the discussion surrounding the ethics of food focuses on consumer practices (Mayes, 2016).

It is at this point of tension between consumer and producer that Michel Foucault's work on biopolitics can be useful. Foucault summarized the dual objective of biopolitics as to "foster life or disallow it to the point of death" (Foucault, 1998, p. 138). Those whose lives have been disallowed are placed outside of the population that is cared for. Under neoliberal approaches to governance, biopolitical strategies increasingly operate through the market and consumer choice. Ethical labels and political consumption are an obvious avenue through which the conduct and behaviours of individuals are made biopolitically salient. Strategies of labelling not only limit ethical and political action to consumption but allow the interests of consumers to set the terms and conditions of whose interests and what practices are considered ethically or politically problematic.

In a series of articles based on their research on the Californian strawberry industry, Julie Guthman and Sandy Brown have noted the biopolitical question of whose lives and interests matter in debates over the use of methyl iodide (Guthman & Brown, 2016a, 2016b, 2016c). They found that much of the debate around the use of this pesticide was framed in terms of consumers' concern for their own health and the health of their families. This is despite the fact that the harmful effects of this pesticide would not affect consumers but would have serious consequences for farm workers. This is a perverse example of "biopolitical sorting" (Guthman & Brown, 2016a, p. 579). Not only was this a valuing of consumer interests over those of farm workers (many of whom were undocumented and thus had little political voice) but, in reality, consumers had no real interest in this issue unless they were showing solidarity with farm workers.

Alternative Consumption?

Consumer activism is partly limited by its reliance on linear and contained conceptualizations of food supply chains that obscure the broader complexes of actors and forces in play. In response, food activists and scholars have promoted an ethic of embracing local and alternative food systems that tries to adopt complex understandings of a food system shaped by a multiplicity of actors and power relations. Alternative food practices are an increasingly prominent solution to problems associated with the global food system, and it is hoped that they can produce an alternative consumer ethic outside market logics.

Alternative food systems are diverse; however, we conceptualize them as seeking to resist the hegemonic forces of globalized and commercialized food regimes. Different manifestations of alternative food can therefore focus on advancing more ecological, more socially just and healthier food systems. A specific example of this is community-supported agriculture (CSA), where there is an attempt to disrupt the conventional consumer–producer relationship.

CSAs operate as an alternative to globalized food systems by promoting direct producer–consumer interactions. Although there is no single CSA model, common to them all is the direct supply of produce from farmers to consumers through subscription arrangements. Generally, under these arrangements, consumers purchase a financial share in a CSA farm in return for a share of the projected harvest over the farm's season. In line with this subscription scheme, CSAs avoid the term "consumer", preferring to speak of "members" or "shareholders" and thus evoke a sense of producer–consumer solidarity. Therefore, while CSAs are diverse, they share the principle of risk-sharing. By opting into a CSA, members commit not only to receiving a share of produce but also to shouldering the risks of production. It is through these direct relationships that alternative food systems are strengthened and ethico-political consumption is enabled.

Despite the strong sense of solidarity achieved through risk-sharing, CSAs are ultimately shaped and limited by consumer interests. The benefits of CSAs for producers are often substantially different to those of consumers. While farmers see the financial benefits of CSAs as consisting in the opportunity to escape the volatile industrial food system, in addition to their "intangible" benefits of education and community-building, consumers are often driven to CSAs through individual desires in relation to taste and quality (Ostrom, 2007, p. 109). This creates an ethical bridge that threatens to destabilize the supposedly "mutual benefit" model of CSAs (Wilkes, 2019). The asymmetry in benefits and motivations leads to a troubled solidarity wherein consumer benefits override producer benefits and often results in exacerbating the challenges faced by farmers in maintaining CSA operations. The consumer self-interest is therefore replicated in alternative systems.

Research shows that the social compact forged between consumer and producer under a CSA model is often broken by the consumer. CSA research in North American and Australian contexts demonstrates significant issues with member attrition. CSA success is often dependent on the ability of a farmer to attract and maintain members. However, for many, a common challenge—and reason for CSA closures—is the inability to maintain long-term member commitment (Brown & Miller, 2008). Ostrom (2007, p. 110) characterizes this as "supermarket withdrawal", suggesting that individuals withdraw from CSAs due to a dislike of the type and quantity of produce delivered. This further underscores the radical monopoly of the supermarket and demonstrates the very fickle reality of consumer solidarity, whereby individual desires override the broader collective goals of CSA practice.

This leads us to question the extent to which alternative consumption such as CSAs are in effect models of "mutual benefit". Through CSAs, we see the repetition of risks to alternative food systems by overplaying the role of consumer ethics. Member attrition of CSAs proves that consumers can remain passive actors rather than active citizens engaged in ethico-political duties. With consumers prioritizing CSAs for individual benefits of taste, the consumer politics of CSAs place producers in the same position as conventional farmers, whose labour is "chronically undervalued" (Ostrom, 2007, p. 107). Thus, even in contexts where the power of the consumer is purportedly deflated, as is the goal of CSA schemes of mutuality, consumer-driven food politics perverts political action by wittingly or unwittingly overstating consumer interests at the centre of food politics.

While alternative practices have much to commend them, we contend they are open to similar criticisms outlined above. This is not to suggest that alternative food systems and practices are equivalent to the global capitalist system. Alternative food systems are important for reasons beyond the consumer. However, we need an approach to food ethics and politics that resists the persistent focus on consumer ethics as means of substantially disrupting food systems, whether global, local or alternative.

Conclusion

The COVID pandemic, floods and droughts associated with a changing climate and famines remind us that the frequency of food-related crises is likely to increase. The capacity to act and reshape our food systems is integral in our response. Our capacity to rethink food systems is unknown; however, we suggest that it will certainly take more than consumer purchasing power. The limits of ethico-political consumption outlined in this chapter demonstrate the need to decentre the consumer as an agent of change. There is little to suggest that framing ethico-political acts as a matter of consumer choice is the solution to holding food corporations and governments to account for their unethical practices. Instead, it becomes clear that such strategies are at risk of considerable co-optation, individualizing ethical action and overstating consumer interests.

Calls for alternative systems are similarly at risk of entanglements with ethico-political consumption. Perhaps alternative food systems provide a vision to disrupt global, industrial food systems. Alternative models of mutuality and community-building, as exemplified in CSAs, can actively disrupt the volatility and passivity of globalized food systems. However, if the consumer continues to be the central agent of change, all alternative models risk falling prey to the same troubles of conventional food ethics. Through producer–consumer relations in CSAs, the illusion of ethico-political consumption is unveiled; that individual choice is enough to lead to systemic disruption and solidarities beyond consumer concern.

There is a desperate need to move beyond a consumer ethics that relegates political action to the supermarket aisles. More research is needed to begin conceptualizing alternative food ethics for future food systems. For now, the current solution of ethico-political consumption falls far short of embracing a necessary and transformative ethic.

References

Arendt, H. (1977). Public rights and private interests: In response to Charles Frankel. In M. M. Mooney (Ed.), *Small comforts for hard times: Humanists on public policy* (pp. 103–108). Columbia University Press.

Arendt, H. (1998). *The human condition* (2nd ed.). University of Chicago Press.

Brown, C., & Miller, S. (2008). The impacts of local markets: A review of research on farmers markets and Community Supported Agriculture (CSA). *American Journal of Agricultural Economics, 90*, 1296–1302.

Carrington, M., Chatzidakis, A., Goworek, H., & Shaw, D. (2021). Consumption ethics: A review and analysis of future directions for interdisciplinary research. *Journal of Business Ethics, 168*(2), 215–238.

Foucault, M. (1998). *The will to knowledge: The history of sexuality, Volume 1* (R. Hurley, Trans.). Penguin Books.

Guthman, J., & Brown, S. (2016a). I will never eat another strawberry again: The biopolitics of consumer-citizenship in the fight against methyl iodide in California. *Agriculture and Human Values, 33*(3), 575–585.

Guthman, J., & Brown, S. (2016b). Midas' not-so-golden touch: On the demise of methyl iodide as a soil fumigant in California. *Journal of Environmental Policy & Planning, 18*(3), 324–341.

Guthman, J., & Brown, S. (2016c). Whose life counts: Biopolitics and the 'bright line' of chloropicrin mitigation in California's strawberry industry. *Science, Technology & Human Values, 41*(3), 461–482.

Illich, I. (1973). *Tools for conviviality.* Harper & Row.
Kantor, A. F. (1976). Upton Sinclair and the Pure Food Drugs Act of 1986: 'I aimed at the public's heart and by accident I hit it in the stomach'. *American Journal of Public Health, 66*(12), 1202–1205.
Klein, N. (2002). *No logo.* Picador.
Mayes, C. (2016). Food at the nexus of bioethics and biopolitics. In M. Rawlinson & C. Ward (Eds.), *The Routledge handbook of food ethics* (1st ed., pp. 167–177). Routledge.
Ostrom, M. R. (2007). Community supported agriculture as an agent of change: Is it working? In T. A. Lyson & C. C. Hinrichs (Eds.), *Remaking the North American food system: Strategies for sustainability* (pp. 112–133). University of Nebraska Press.
Soper, K., & Trentmann, F. (Eds.). (2008). *Citizenship and consumption.* Palgrave Macmillan.
Wells, T. (2016). Free choice is informed choice: Why we need ethical warning labels on animal products. *ABC Religion & Ethics*, June 2. Retrieved June 3, 2020, from https://www.abc.net.au/religion/free-choice-is-informed-choice-why-we-need-ethical-warning-label/10096936
Wilkes, B. A. (2019). *A snapshot of community supported agriculture in Australia and Aotearoa New Zealand 2018: Preliminary descriptive results.* Australian National University. Retrieved July 30, 2021, from https://openresearch-repository.anu.edu.au/bitstream/1885/164046/3/A%20snapshot%20of%20CSA%20in%20Australia%20and%20Aotearoa%20New%20Zealand%202018.pdf

CHAPTER 13

Afterword: Temporary Measures

Alex Blanchette

Abstract The disruptions that wracked food supply chains amid the COVID-19 pandemic were not exceptional circumstances so much as they were events that intensified and clarified the routine norms of a capitalist system of sustenance that operates in a state of permanent emergency. The capitalist food system is one that develops through temporary measures—acts that seek to patch structural weaknesses before they explode in ways that could destabilize the system itself. Looking via the lens of US animal agriculture, this concluding chapter asks if viewing the food system in this way might open up alternative ways of thinking about political agency in times of mundane crisis, highlighting the messy contingencies of capitalism's own persistent efforts to foreclose the realizations of other, fuller visions of nourishment.

Keywords Food system • Capitalism • Structural weaknesses • Supply chains • US animal agribusiness

A. Blanchette (✉)
Tufts University, Medford, MA, USA
e-mail: alex.blanchette@tufts.edu

V. Stead, M. Hinkson (eds.), *Beyond Global Food Supply Chains*,
https://doi.org/10.1007/978-981-19-3155-0_13

The preceding chapters depict a world of food commodities beset by ubiquitous disruption, even as the fundamental conditions of an ever-colonizing capitalism change little over time. Moments of rupture and friction that would appear to unsettle capitalist hegemony paradoxically entrench it even deeper (Giles). Declarations of looming emergency become development tools to ensure food chains attract and accumulate yet more capital (Sippel). Constant disruptions to ecology and livelihood discipline agriculturalists to resigned acquiescence (Rickards and Hinkson). Invocations of crisis seek further investment in the status quo (Masco, 2017). As Victoria Stead and Kirstie Petrou demonstrate, elemental honorary titles like "essential" fall flat when they are emplaced onto the farmers, farm workers and food supply chain workers who sustain our lives. Rather than a stable essence to be protected, maintained and nurtured over time, the authors of this volume collectively paint a food system marked by what Melinda Cooper (2008, p. 20) has called a capitalist delirium restlessly defined by the cyclical "breakdown and recreation of whole worlds". As Tomaso Ferrando and others argue, the disruptions that wracked food supply chains amid the COVID-19 pandemic were not exceptional circumstances so much as they were events that intensified and clarified the routine norms of a capitalist system of sustenance that operates in a state of permanent emergency.

Inspired by these chapters, my concluding suggestion is to consider the capitalist food system as one that develops through temporary measures (see Stead and Petrou)—and that perhaps agri-capitalism is itself best seen as a massive temporary measure. A temporary measure is an act that seeks to patch a structural weakness before it explodes in a way that could destabilize the system itself; temporary measures are, more simply, makeshift solutions to a problem. The sweeping and much-publicized shifts to trade and labour policy that tried to salve scarcity, wastage and livelihood ruination during the COVID-19 pandemic appear, in this light, as something of a ruse. As Henry and Morris illuminate, these rapid shifts in governance were not merely a reflection of exceptional circumstances. The management of any supply chain, they suggest, is one of unending adjustment as issues large and small erupt to the surface; even in "normal" times, the labour of supply chains is not characterized by frictionless execution but instead by constant patching. The spectacular quality of COVID-19 policy adjustments merely made governance through temporary measures more visible. What I find useful about focusing onto temporary measures is that it might open up alternative ways of thinking about political agency in times of mundane crisis. Seeing the food system as a patchwork of temporary measures helps us not only sense the contingent messiness of these processes but also allows us to question the idea that capitalist sustenance is directed by omniscient, rational agents. Appearing less like all-powerful planners, corporate financiers and international policymakers emerge in these chapters as fundamentally reactive: desperately trying to keep afloat capitalist food worlds.

I approach this volume, and its analyses of the non-transformational upheavals of COVID-19, through my own experiences working in US animal agribusinesses. A decade prior to this pandemic, I spent eight months shadowing managers across their activities in one of the world's largest pork corporations—a network that annually births, raises and kills some 7,000,000 hogs for global distribution. These managers' days consisted of tamping down endemic crises—their every moment of work was directed towards mending problems that stemmed from their own ambitions to confine millions of immunocompromised and genetically homogenous animals in a patch of land. Even at the corporation's upper echelons, time was not primarily spent plotting future models and visions of increased capital accumulation. It was directed towards devising temporary measures to keep this biological experiment afloat (see Blanchette, 2020). At a moment when agri-food corporations project themselves as smoothly occupying and stitching together the entire planet, it is time to take more seriously the fragility and even the pathetic nature of how food firms maintain a hold on life (Lien, 2015; Blanchette, 2018).

At the same time, and as these chapters suggest, there is a certain recursive power that comes with governing through temporary measures. The five largest North American capitalist meat-production firms alone sickened 59,000 of their employees with COVID-19—and they have killed no fewer than 269 people since March 2020 (Hassan, 2021). By invoking the *Defense Production Act*—itself a temporary measure—in April 2020 to legally insulate these companies from prosecution, then-president Donald Trump declared these (largely migrant) workers sacrifices to national infrastructure. The perversity of this temporary measure, this most astonishing and latest temporary measure, is that it effectively excused all of the harmful temporary measures that preceded this state-sanctioned licence to kill. Consider that *prior* to the emergence of COVID-19, US animal agribusiness was a patchwork of slaughterhouse-line speed-limit exceptions, special rules put in place to accommodate growing animal herd sizes and that allowed select companies to strain human bodies to the point where debilitating repetitive-motion injuries were routine. As US confined animal feeding operations have grown in scale and concentration since the 1980s, they have been permitted to operate through special laws that exempt them from regulation under "normal" industrial rules governing air pollution and emissions standards (see Blanchette, 2019). Even animal breeding farms, with their erotic methods of artificial insemination that help increase productivity, had to pursue unique agricultural legal exceptions from state legislatures to keep them from running afoul of bestiality laws (Rosenberg, 2017). North American meat production has long developed by exceeding moral and legal norms and then pursuing temporary measures that enable it to continue unaltered. But the temporary measures put into place during COVID-19 make all these prior acts seem innocuous compared to the current fact that people were killed for corporate profits (see also Dickinson).

From where I write and live, in the United States, this history of agricultural capitalism has been a matter of ever-compounding brutalities that (for some) make the foundational horrors of that country, with its white-washed settler-colonial family farms, seem like an object of nostalgic longing. Yet this is where I read the chapters of this volume as making a profound intervention. A sub-thread of these chapters is that the status quo of settler-productivist agriculture is itself the problem (see Donati, Altman and Markham). What sets this volume's chapters apart is not simply their timely depictions of the even-further-destabilized capitalist food system on which so many depend. It is their refusal to play into the structural logic of temporary measures, insisting that agri-capitalism's fundamental drive is its own continued reproduction through the suppression of indigenous and other lifeways and relations to land that promise the realization of other worlds. On this score, they remind me of a political philosophy articulated by the socialist-feminist theorist Silvia Federici (1998). Federici calls the rise of liberal capitalism—and its restless spread across natural and moral borders—a *counter-revolution*. She insists that the emergence of capitalism was not a historical break from European feudalism—not a new chapter in a linear progressive march forward in historical time—but instead a *reactionary* means of subduing ordinary peoples' yearnings for new forms of equality and experimental sociality that threatened to unmake feudalism's racial-patriarchal mooring (see also Robinson, 2021). What these chapters insist, not unlike Federici, is that capitalism is itself better seen as a massive temporary measure whose delirious disruptions continually block and misdirect the pursuit of fuller visions of nourishment throughout the food system. In so doing, they prod us to nurture ways of living and acting with the realization, as Di Haggerty declares in Kelly Donati's chapter, with respect to the idea that settler private property and productivism is soon to be eclipsed, that "We're only here temporarily".

References

Blanchette, A. (2018). Nothing new. *Journal for the Anthropology of North America, 21*(2), 72–73.

Blanchette, A. (2019). Living waste and the labor of toxic health on American factory farms. *Medical Anthropology Quarterly, 33*(1), 80–100.

Blanchette, A. (2020). *Porkopolis: American animality, standardized life, and the factory farm*. Duke University Press.

Cooper, M. (2008). *Life as surplus: Biotechnology and capitalism in the neoliberal era*. University of Washington Press.

Federici, S. (1998). *Caliban and the witch: Women, the body, and primitive accumulation*. Autonomedia.

Hassan, A. (2021, October 28). Covid hit U.S. meat plants far harder than thought. *The New York Times*. https://www.nytimes.com/2021/10/28/world/meatpacking-workers-covid-cases-deaths.html

Lien, M. (2015). *Becoming salmon: Aquaculture and the domestication of a fish*. University of California Press.

Masco, J. (2017). The crisis in crisis. *Current Anthropology, 58*(S15), S65–S76.

Robinson, C. (2021). *Black Marxism: The making of the black radical tradition* (3rd ed.). University of North Carolina Press.

Rosenberg, G. (2017). How meat changed sex: The law of interspecies intimacy after industrial reproduction. *GLQ, 23*(4), 473–507.

Index

V. Stead, M. Hinkson (eds.), *Beyond Global Food Supply Chains*,
https://doi.org/10.1007/978-981-19-3155-0

FSC
www.fsc.org
MIX
Papier | Fördert
gute Waldnutzung
FSC® C083411

Kolibri 360 GmbH
Ferdinand-Jühlke-Straße 7
99095 Erfurt, Deutschland
produktsicherheit@kolibri360.de